Venusian Health Magic And Venusian Secret - Science

SPECIAL INTRODUCTION BY TIMOTHY GREEN BECKLEY

Direct Communications From The Space Brothers
Two Classic Books in One!
- UPDATED -

MICHAEL X BARTON

VENUSIAN HEALTH MAGIC
AND
VENUSIAN SECRET SCIENCE

BY

MICHAEL X

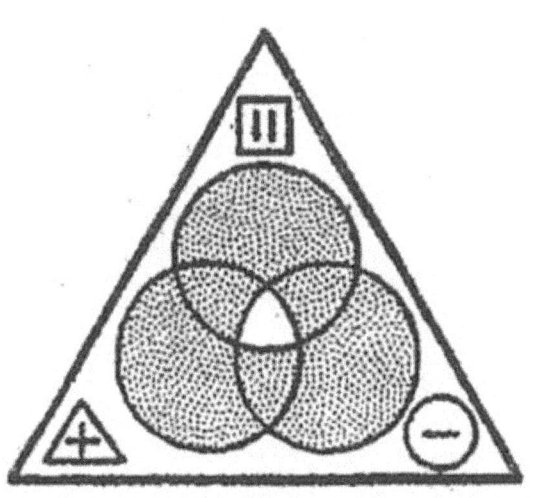

INNER LIGHT/GLOBAL COMMUNICATIONS

Venusian Health Magic and Venusian Secret Science

By Michael X Barton – With Special Introduction By Timothy Green Beckley

Copyright © 2017 - Timothy Green Beckley DBA Inner Light/ Global Communications,
Originally Published in 1959 by Futura Press

All Rights Reserved

Nonfiction - Printed in the United States of America

No part of this book may be reproduced, stored in retrieval system or transmitted in any form or by any means, electronic, mechanical, photocopying, recording, without express permission of the publisher.

Timothy Green Beckley: Editorial Director
Carol Rodriguez: Publishers Assistant
Editor and Layout: Tim R. Swartz,
Sean Casteel: Associate Editor,
William Kern: Editorial Assistant

Front and Back Cover Art By Carol Ann Rodriguez

For free catalog write:
Global Communications
P.O. Box 753
New Brunswick, NJ 08903

Free Subscription to Conspiracy Journal E-Mail Newsletter: www.conspiracyjournal.com

Email: mrufo8@hotmail.com

THIS is an Educational and Inspirational Course of Study dealing with interplanetary subjects. It is especially written and intended for NEW AGE individuals everywhere. Statements in this Course are based on Scientific and Super-Sensory Findings. No claim is made as to what the information cited may do in any given case and the publishers assume no obligation for opinions expressed or implied by the author.

CONTENTS

MESSAGES FROM OTHER WORLDS - THE LESSONS TO BE LEARNED 6
AUTHOR'S FORWARD 13
Part 1. WHEN A GOOD BODY BREAKS 15
Part 2. CONTACTING THE VENUSIANS 29
Part 3. THREE RIVERS TO CROSS 41
Part 4. HOW TO GIVE UP YOUR ILLS 57
Part 5. THE MAGICAL "LIFETRONS" 69
Part 6. POLISHING A LIVING PYRAMID 87
Part 7. RAISING THE TRUE CAPSTONE 101
Part 8. MODULATING YOURSELF UPWARD 111
Part 9. MAGIC OF THE GOLDEN SPHERE 125
Part 10. VENUSIAN VRIL AND VITALITY 133

VENUSIAN SECRET-SCIENCE 153

AUTHOR'S FORWARD 157
1. COMMUNICATING WITH VENUS 161
2. THE COSMIC PLAN REVEALED 185
3. CHOSEN BY THE WISE ONES 207
4. YOUR GRADUATION PROM EARTH 233
5. YOUR MAGIC LIFE ON VENUS 255
6. VENUSIAN SECRET POWERS 281
7. THE BEINGS BEYOND VENUS 305

How Michael X Contacts The Space-Beings! 320

Supplementary Instructions..330

MESSAGES FROM OTHER WORLDS – THE LESSONS TO BE LEARNED
By Timothy Green Beckley

REST assured, Michael X was one of the great avatars of the early UFO/New Age movement of the 1950s, best known and highly respected throughout the high desert country of southern California.

The popular mystic spoke with great articulation and sincerity at many of the well attended outdoor conventions held annually at Giant Rock, a private landing strip just out of Joshua Tree in the broiling hot Mohave Desert, where temperatures often run above a hundred degrees by high noon.

To his credit, Michael X spoke calmly and collectively about the arrival of the silvery spaceships, dubbed flying saucers, explaining how they were piloted by friendly space beings from this solar system and way beyond. On a mission of peace and harmony, Michael hailed the arrival of the Space Brotherhood whom he believed were materializing here to offer assistance in any way possible to elevate our consciousness to a more harmonious one. Their goal? Allowing us to join the cosmic league of nations, a federation of spiritually advanced worlds who exist all around us in this and other dimensions, whether we believe it or not! I guess you could call Michael X a guru of sorts, though he didn't head a religious cult nor was he looking to attract a fanatical following in the manner of other more self absorbent "masters" of universal wisdom. No! Michael X was an avatar in the true sense of the word – an advocate for all of humanity. So that he didn't become part of a cult of personality, Michael refused to reveal his last name but added the X after his first name as sort of a symbol that represented all of the mysteries of our world and the space and time we inhabit, even if we had not officially acknowledge the legitimacy of others hob knobbing among the stars.

Short in stature, but a giant in his thinking, little is known or has been written about Michael X's background. We do know his last name was Barton, and he was a salesman before being engulfed with the UFO contactee movement. I did speak to him once but he never would reveal anything about his past, preferring to let his "accomplishments" speak for themselves. If one owned a complete collection of Michael X's monographs, which I estimate number around 25 and were self published by his Futura Press from roughly 1956 through the late 60s or early 70s, one might be able to put together some incomplete biographical notes. We know that Michael Barton was residing in Los Angeles when he found his life changed, when his best friend Jim became very ill with a condition that baffled the best doctors.

While meditating over his buddy's deteriorating condition, Michael found he was able to receive telepathic communications beamed to him from more advanced cosmic souls. Not wanting to alienate his business clients, but desperate to get the information he had collected out to a growing number of adherents in UFO and New Age philosophy, he began to self-publish courses and monographs under the pseudonym of Michael X. His work was read and distributed widely as believers and skeptics alike instinctively took to what he had to say and recognized the importance of its content. You see, Michael X didn't just write about lights in the sky – or about close encounters for that matter. No, Michael X got his information first hand via telepathy from his extraterrestrial "guides." And they taught him much, everything from health secrets to how their understanding of science, philosophy and religion, could possibly propel us forward into a New Age of reason and enlightenment. And above all else – Michael X shared what he learned from the "Venusians" – whom he said were his closest acquaintances – in a series of very concise study guides which he sold mainly at UFO and metaphysical meetings, but also advertised in publications like Fate and Ray Palmer's *Flying Saucers From Outer Space magazine*".

In fact, truth be told, I was selling Michael X's books when I was 15. We would advertise them in our little mimeographed publications, and Michael would drop ship them to our readers. He had books on cosmic telepathy, how to initiate contact with the UFOnauts, health secrets, visions at Fatima, Nazi UFO secrets and so forth. Before he vanished from the scene he sold most of his books to Gray Barker of Saucerian Press. When Barker passed I purchased all the remaining copies and had them lying around in various cubbyholes for years but now feel it is important for these monographs to be brought back into circulation.

I do not know if Michael X is still with us or not. If he is I know he will not be resentful of the fact that we have decided to compile and reissue some of his most vital writings for an entirely new generation to consume and gain knowledge from. We have already reprinted his work Flying Saucer Revelations as a bonus section in the book **"Vi Venus: Starchild,"** now obtainable directly from us or off Amazon.com.

Truth is his books were more than just simple discourses and mere New Age chit chat. Some of them, like the book you are now holding contained vital lessons – lessons he had taken down directly from his Space Brother friends who saw the necessity in sharing some of their knowledge with earth dwellers so as to hasten their development and improve the quality of their life both physically and mentally.

To expedite the release of this important cosmic message to all of human kind, we have combined **Venusian Secret Society** and **Venusian Health Science** into one large volume. Though originally published in the 1950s and 1960s it never received the distribution it should have. A limited printing was made available which sold mainly to his Los Angeles-based students and those who were lucky enough to catch his rare public appearances at the Giant Rock conventions. In fact, though we have hunted high and low we have been unable at this point to find any photographs that might exist of him either on stage or off. Readers who might have a snap shot or two in their private collection will hopefully share them with us so that we may post them on line.

At one point we obtained Michael's private contact number from the late Dr Frank E. Stranges who is best known for his purported contact with a "stranger" from another world who lived for three years inside the Pentagon," Val Thor said he was a visitor here from the inside of the planet Venus. We spoke to Michael briefly at his home but he didn't seem anxious to communicate with the outside world as he once did. We later discovered that he had undergone a bone chilling experience in which he was almost killed when he was set up by the "dark forces," who told him to go to a particular spot in the desert for an important meeting. Luckily he was warned by the "boys from topside" who were his long time friends, to get back into his vehicle at the last moment, just before he saw the sun glimmering off the barrow of a firearm that was being aimed at him from a short distance behind a boulder in the desert.

We suspect this assassination attempt had something to do with his belief that at least some UFOs were constructed under the guidance of Nazi engineers and scientists at the end of World War II, when these same war criminals were escorted into the U.S. and made citizens under the highly controversial Project Paperclip, while some of their criminal associates were being rightfully put to death back in Germany. Being a Nazi scientist supposedly made them better than the next SS official who did not slip out of Berlin under the cover of darkness and with the proper credentials which would make them free here in America. Michael X's tract **"We Want You,"** originally came out around 1962 (not to be confused with the edition on sale on line which is not authorized) and was later reissued by Saucerian Press in 1969. A couple of years ago we put together some of Michael's "briefing papers." ***Trilogy of the Unknown*** goes into some detail about the propulsion system of the Nazi generated flying saucers, why the aliens will not let us set up bases on the moon and a discussion of the top secret underground community located at the South Pole known as Rainbow City.

Michael X was a welcome speaker at the annual Giant Rock UFO Conventions held just outside Joshua Tree, CA in the desert.

While the talks by Michael X and others were going on, it was not unusual for a UFO to be spotted nearby at the Giant Rock convention.

WORDS OF UNIVERSAL KNOWLEDGE AND ENLIGHTENMENT

Over the years I have received letters and calls from those who were touched by Michael X's teachings. They were very upset that he had vanished from the scene and could not be reached, as they were looking for further guidance so that they could travel along the same path to spiritual enlightenment.

The below communication is representative of the type of mail that crossed my desk.

In about 1965 I had the privilege to listen to Michael X. Barton give a lecture at the "*San Antonio Street College Of Metaphysics Enquiry*". Michael was a very small man and was well dressed. After the lecture I asked in private what the X. meant in his name. He said that it was in respect to Christ. Later on I had the pleasure of meeting Dr. Wallace Halsey's beautiful wife by the name of Tarna Halsey.

(JW my guru and teacher once told me that Wallace and his wife were at the "Giant Rock UFO Convention" and Wallace was talking and walking around with a space man who looked the person. Tarna came up and told them that she was going to take a picture of both of them together. The space person told Tarna that if she took a picture of them that his image wouldn't show on the print. This was due to the fact that they had been talking about very high vibrational thoughts that his picture wouldn't show up. Tarna then said, "I have a very good camera and I'll be able to get your picture." She took the picture and the space person couldn't be seen. He then tried to tell her that he had told her what had happened. Later on Tarna came back to her husband and the space person told Tarna that she could take their picture, and he would be able to be seen on the picture. She then took another picture and the space person came out on the picture, because they had been talking about normal things. I later had an interview with Tarna and she said that she had demonstrated to a friend that she could become invisible to a camera. She was able to do this with her friend. She in a previous life was from Venus. She later became the wife of "The Crusher" who was a retired wrestler. The "Crusher" was on the radio at times with Herb Jepko on his telephone talk show coming from Salt Lake City.

We agree that Michael X could be thought of as a provocative individual, however it can also be said that he was a great visionary. Though the words in this book are said to have been "projected to earth" by advanced space beings, even if they were not their value can hardly be contested.

Our mantra for this Michael X work is READ AND LEARN! –

YouTube Channel – Mr UFOs Secret Files - Over 170 videos posted

https://www.youtube.com/user/MRUFO1100

www.ConspiracyJournal.com

Author's Forward

"*VENUSIAN HEALTH MAGIC*" contains a wealth of vital instruction and inspiration for all of you wonderful souls who have come to know that you are never alone# Intelligence and love direct the universe, and always are "at your service" to lift you upward into a healthier, happier and higher vibration.

Our Space Brothers—The Venusians—tell us that no one on earth need be sick, or wracked with pain, or filled with a hopeless despair IF the amazing health principles they have unselfishly brought to us, are practiced.

The "Health Magic" of the Planetary Teachers is intended for all of us earthlings who have a burning desire to leave poor health behind us forever, and go on to wonderful Joys and activities that come only to the healthy. Due to the fact that the Venusians are much further advanced in their understanding of man than we are, they have learned all about the electric power that makes the human body function as it does. Ihey discovered that radiant health and vitality could be stepped up by the simple means of increasing one's intake of Life Electricity, through a positive diet of highly vitalized foods, and by a conscious direction of what they call "Lifetrons".

You will learn of these and many other life-giving discoveries in the pages that follow. They will open NEW VISTAS for you in your search for health and mastery. Thrilling adventures are just ahead for you and for all those who travel the path of ever-increasing LIFE...leading to the STARS!

MICHAEL X

Seer of the New Age

WHEN A GOOD BODY BREAKS
Part One

THE best way I know of to relay to you the life-giving health secrets of the Venusians, so that you will be able to apply them most effectively in your own life, is by telling you of a certain remarkable experience. Jim Lindy, a good friend of mine whom I have known for many years, was the nucleus around which this most unusual experience revolved. It was through my knowing Jim, and whole-heartedly responding to his sincere and desperate call for help, that I was plunged into a tremendous New Age adventure with the Space People of Venus.

I hadn't seen Jim Lindy since 1953 when he and I had been active together in forming an "Interplanetary Contact Group" in Washington State. The group was small, but what it lacked in size it made up for in sincere earnestness and enthusiasm. We used Jim's spacious house for our meetings, which were held several times a month.

As you may have already guessed, the purpose of our little group was to learn everything we possibly could about "Flying Saucers" and to contact the Space People themselves, for their knowledge of the universe was evidently not only far greater than our own, but based on spiritual principles as yet unrecognized by most or Earth's people.

Some of us made splendid progress in understanding these things which, to the average "man on the street" seemed then to be fantastically strange and highly improbable to say the least. Our burning desire was to learn how we might increase our awareness of that which is above and beyond the ordinary, and by systematic steps, gradually "attune" ourselves to the higher vibrations of the Space People. We

THIS SIDE FOR STUDENT NOTES

were confident and hopeful that in due time the proper methods would be discovered whereby we could make actual contact with them.

Jim Lindy was by nature a spiritually progressive individual, open-minded to the Nth degree. Yet by no manner of means could he be considered in the least gullible. He had seen several "UFOs" himself in the night skies and had been filled with awe and wonderment at the sight. On one occasion a brilliantly glowing object of huge proportions, was sighted in the sky near the vicinity of his own home. It circled the area twice, and then with amazing acceleration, the bright object climbed straight upward several thousand feet and headed in the direction of the horizon at unbelievable speed. Jim was so profoundly impressed by what he had been permitted to witness (no Saucer sighting happens by "accident") that he determined to do all within his power to find out more about the unique and marvelously intelligent beings who make their home on worlds far distant from this Earth

In the latter part of 1953 I left the Interplanetary Contact Group in the very capable hands of Jim Lindy and moved from Washington State to Southern California to carry out some important plans I had for further investigating the UFO phenomena. I heard from Jim by letter every so often, and his reports of the group's progress were encouraging and hopeful.

One of the nicest things about Jim is his constant optimism and cheerfulness. He radiated this good feeling in his letters and it was a joy to receive any communication from him.

In 1955, his letters suddenly took a negative turn.

Jim began to convey a depressed note, as if he had for some reason become deeply discouraged. Finally one letter contained really bad news. For "private reasons" Jim had resigned from active leadership or the group. However, he was not disbanding the group, but had turned over its leadership to another member and they were still holding meetings at his house although much less frequently than before.

After this news, no further word came from Jim Lindy for over a year. Concluding that he had somehow lost interest in the group's original purpose, and that his desire to contact the Space People had waned, I kept on in a quiet but steady fashion with my own studies and research. Then, very early one morning I was startled by a quick knock at my door and a loud voice calling out "Telegram! Telegram!" When I opened the door, the messenger thrust the following telegram into my hands:

THIS SIDE FOR STUDENT NOTES

ARRIVING LOS ANGELES AIRPORT TONIGHT 6:00 – STOP

CAN YOU MEET ME? – STOP

URGENTLY IMPORTANT MATTER – STOP

JIM LINDY

At once I turned the telegram over and wrote the following reply to my friend:

AFFIRMATIVE - STOP

SEE YOU AT 6:00 P.M. - STOP

MICHAEL X

That evening I drove out to the airport and joined the little crowd of those who were eagerly "standing by" to see the 6:00 o'clock plane land, and taxi up to the gate with its load of passengers. My mind was filled now with the vivid image of Jim Lindy as he had been in 1953, trim-waisted, straight shouldered, vital and strong. Of course, he would look a little different than when I had last seen him...possibly a trifle more mature, but with the same beaming smile I remembered as distinctly his own.

I was due for a severe shock. When the plane came to a atop and the passengers began streaming out, an entirely different looking Jim Lindy than the one I had been picturing a moment before, made his way toward me in the crowd. His face was tired and haggard. His hair, which formerly was jet black and luxuriantly thick, had turned grayish-white and was quite thin in spots. The trim waist was gone. A "pot-belly" replaced it. The shoulders were stooped and the old-time smile was very different. It was more like a grimace of pain.

I MEET A VERY SICK MAN WHOSE CONDITION HAS BAFFLED DOCTORS.

I greeted Jim with all the good cheer I could muster for the occasion, and after hustling him into my car, drove swiftly toward the section of Los Angeles in which my apartment is located. On the way, Jim expressed a desire to talk. After saying how grateful he was to have me meet him at the airport and telling a little about his flight, he came to the crux of the matter.

"As you see, Michael, I'm a physical wreck. For the past two years my health has been on a downhill toboggan slide until now I'm at the point of losing all hope. Completely out of the clear blue sky my stomach started 'acting up'. Naturally I went

THIS SIDE FOR STUDENT NOTES

to a doctor for a checkup and medicines, but still my stomach trouble stayed with me. In fact, it got worse.

"Treatments I took only seemed to aggravate it. Then, to make matters even worse and more bewildering I began to feel pain intermittently in my gall-bladder, liver and appendix. You can imagine how upset I became over all these physical ills."

"Yes, Jim, I can. And I can also imagine that these various pains were leading you to become better acquainted with your inner anatomy. A most unpleasant way to learn about it. But what did you do then?" I asked sympathetically.

"The usual thing," Jim replied, "when one doctor failed to help me I went to another, and then another, until I had made the rounds of a great many of them. One doctor thought I had liver trouble, another said it was kidney stones, others said gall bladder trouble, but none were sure of just what was the main trouble. They took a lot of X-rays for which I spent a good deal of money, but discovered nothing definite. One specialist suggested an 'exploratory operation' but I balked. You know how I have always felt about such things."

"Yes," I responded, "if you've always believed that if there were any other way to avoid being operated on you'd try it first and consent to being cut open only if there was no other possible solution to the problem."

Jim Lindy looked at me and nodded his head in agreement. After a long pause he spoke.

"I held off' bringing my troubles to you until the very last moment. But when my health problems became steadily worse, and all the usual doctoring methods—the pills wonder drugs, X-rays and health devices—failed to restore my good health, I began to feel that my condition was becoming really serious. I not only feel weak and miserable most of the time, but I have aged considerably in the past two years. Physically I'm at a very low ebb. Mentally, I'm far from being the keen-eyed man I was. As a result, I've made more than a few unwise decisions in my business that have cost me a great deal of needless expense. Now that so much of my money has been spent on doctoring with no improvement in my condition, I'm worried about not being able to earn enough money to keep on with health treatments. It looks hopeless."

"You've overlooked one important avenue of help," I said as I turned my car off the freeway and headed for my apartment in the suburbs.

THIS SIDE FOR STUDENT NOTES

I glanced quickly at Jim and noted a glint of hope in his eye.

"What do you mean?" he queried.

"The Space People," I said bluntly.

"You've seen the Saucers just as I have. I know you believe the spacecraft are controlled by intelligent beings from outer space who must be far wiser than the majority of doctors on earth. It might just be possible the Space People have access to knowledge and healing methods far in advance of any we now have. Considering that these beings have superior intelligence and understanding, your case wouldn't appear at all hopeless. They probably would be able to get results that to us might even seem miraculous."

I didn't tell Jim then that I had been successful in my long-time quest—that for the past year I had been privileged to make actual contact with two of the most wondrous and noble beings I have ever seen—Lon-Zara and Shelana, of Venus. These advanced human beings, for such they were, had long ago "graduated" from Earth to the planet Venus, and are actively engaged in two fields or service.

One: they hold important positions in the Lifetronic Healing Center on Venus, Lon-Zara being a master healer. And Shelana is his most valuable assistant in the great work.

Two: they have a limited number of NEW AGE students living on our planet Earth, with whom they are in frequent contact by telepathy and other means.

Thus, a network of key individuals comprised of men and women in various fields of human service on earth are secretly instructed by the Venusians who become their Cosmic Teachers. And, by releasing certain higher phases of knowledge to the Key men and women of Earth at such times as that knowledge is most needed, the Masters of Venus assist greatly in lessening the suffering or Earth's humanity, and uplifting all of us into a more positive vibration.

Lon-Zara, when last he had communicated with me telepathically, had taught me many astounding facts regarding the wonderful health and amazing longevity of the people of Venus.

To a true student of the occult or hidden side of life, none of the Venusian Secret Science is the least bit "impractical" or even fantastic. You and I know that all higher teachings of life are far more practical and true than the mere human mind can

THIS SIDE FOR STUDENT NOTES

realize at first. In time, as the personal vibrations become raised into higher and still higher octaves of being, all limitations vanish, and man's Spirit controls matter.

Those of you who have studied "**VENUSIAN SECRET SCIENCE**" in which I related my series of contacts with Lon-Zara, know that he gave me special suggestions to observe in regard to the NEW AGE diet as well as other matters. By applying those suggestions and "sticking with them" until they became positive habits in my daily life, I discovered to my great joy that my health improved immensely. But that was not the only practical benefit. My mental and spiritual faculties became much keener and more active than ever before. This has been a great blessing to me, for today I am a more awakened channel for NEW AGE TRUTH than I had ever dreamed was possible.

By sharing what I have received with those who are hungry for this knowledge, my whole life has blossomed beyond belief. Now, I felt I must share some of this health and joy with Jim Lindy, and as quickly as possible.

"You talk as if you really know more about the Space People than you're letting on." Jim remarked.

"I am willing to try anything that doesn't conflict with reason, and as you well know, I for one am open-minded on the subject of Space People. Maybe they can help me, provided you and I are fortunate enough to contact them. I know they exist, whoever 'they' might be, for I've seen their ships in the sky. But unless we're lucky, or use really effective methods, it will take some time to get my 'call for help' through to them."

What Jim said pleased me. Already his mental attitude was more positive and hopeful. Moreover, he was sincere in his desire to get well, and was not at all dismayed by the thought—unique as it must have seemed to him—that the wise and powerful beings from a far distant world might be able to assist him to recover a very precious possession which he had somehow lost...namely his good health.

We arrived at my apartment dwelling within thirty minutes from the time we left the airport. It is a large apartment, not new, but well constructed and designed for human comfort and convenience. The rooms are large and cheerfully decorated. My housekeeper, Lenore, occupies another apartment in the same vicinity.

She is a gentle and gracious soul, deeply interested in the advanced teachings of the Venusians. By putting their teachings into practice in her own life, Lenore has succeeded in outwitting to a great extent, the effects of Father Time.

THIS SIDE FOR STUDENT NOTES

She is very youthful looking. In her estimation, mere calendar years are of little importance. The thing that matters most is biological age, the flexibility or one's cells and arteries. By true standards Lenore is indeed young.

I showed Jim into the living room and we relaxed in comfortable lounge chairs while we talked. It was apparent that Jim was exceedingly tired and in need of a long rest. His health had indeed broken, and it would take time to mend it.

"Can you get a leave of absence for three months?" I asked him."It will take about that long for us to carry out certain experiments I have in mind for contacting the Venusians. You can stay here as my guest and enjoy a well deserved rest in this pleasant environment. We haven't seen each other in years, and three months vacation here will give us time to renew our friendship as well as contact the Space People and get you on your feet again. I've a spare room here for you and your stay will cost next to nothing. We can both bask in the California sunshine until we are as brown and healthy as a couple of Hawaiian natives.

With perceptible emotion, Jim accepted the invitation, and it seemed as though a great burden had suddenly lifted from his shoulders. Only a few moments before he had been at his wit's end, and now a true and natural way was opening for him when almost all hope and personal finances were gone. I knew how he felt, for I too had once been in a similar position and had received help from unexpected sources. It is all part of the working out of a great spiritual law. What we give out comes back to us, in increased measure, though not always from the direction in which we expect it to come.

The friendly jingle of a bell told us that dinner was now on the table and waiting for us in the dining room. As we took our places at the table, I could not help wondering how Jim would react to the New Age dietary ideas that we practiced.

But when I noted the delighted expression on his face after he had tasted the wholesome, all-natural and delicious fruit salad which Lenore placed before him, I knew Jim would not only enjoy his food, but would greatly benefit; for a vital, natural diet is Earthman's first step in preparing himself physically and spiritually to meet the Space People.

THIS SIDE FOR STUDENT NOTES

CONTACTING THE VENUSIANS
Part Two

AFTER our dinner of delicious, natural foods, I was pleased to hear Jim say that he had never imagined this kind of food could be so satisfying and sustaining as well as appetizing. We thanked Lenore for having served two hungry men such a delightful feast, and then enjoyed a few moments of relaxing conversation before bedtime. Jim was looking forward eagerly to the great experience of contacting the highly intelligent Space People..He sensed somehow that with my aid he would be able to achieve his life-long dream of actually meeting the Wise ones.

Not wishing to over-tire him, I soon brought the conversation to a close and accompanied Jim to the guest room where I bade him "good night" and then retired to my own room for my usual deep and refreshing sleep. Before going to sleep, however, I relaxed as completely as possible, and concentrated my thoughts upon Lon-Zara, the Venusian master healer whom I knew to be my Cosmic Teacher. It was entirely possible that "L" was already aware of Jim Lindy's critical health problem. The Space People have their own surprising ways of keeping well informed, especially on any matters relating to the welfare and progress of their students. However, I thought it advisable to notify "L" of Jim's earnest desire to regain his health.

Quietly I followed my regular procedure of stilling my mind, raising the vibratory rate of my psychic brain centers (pituitary and pineal glands) by placing psychic gems (Telolith and Lapis Lingua) directly over those centers and exerting a mild pressure with my hands. I then visualized a white beam of light shining from the center of my forehead toward Venus. On this beam of light I sent out my call to the Master Lon-Zara, and patiently awaited his response to the message.

THIS SIDE FOR STUDENT NOTES

A minute passed. Two minutes. Then I suddenly felt the same strange sensation that invariably happens whenever a message is sent to me from the Space people. I can only partially describe it by saying that it is a physical, mental and spiritual feeling of "at-one-ment" with another living, thinking, human being whose vibrations are extraordinarily harmonious.

As his dynamic thoughts are conveyed one by one to my mind, I feel a sense of unsual peace, harmony, joyous stimulation and timelessness. For a few precious moments, time ceases to be, and I am strongly aware only of his magnetic presence, his "consciousness" and the living truth of his vital message. Briefly, this is the feeling of "attunement" that came to me after I had sent out my call to Lon-Zara.

With this feeling there came also into my awareness the special musical tone (in Key of D) with which Lon-Zara makes his presence known to me by Telethot. His masterful thoughts followed the musical tone:

"Greetings, Michael X! Blessings of Life, Love and ever-increasing Light to you and all our loved ones on planet Earth. Once again it is our privilege and Joy to serve our Earth Brothers and Sisters, and assist them in their upward evolution. You, beloved brother, were right in reasoning that we already know of the serious illness of your dear friend, Jim Lindy. We have been aware of his plight for some time, but it was not until recently that we could act in his behalf without interfering with his own will. Fortunately, Jim Lindy is open-minded regarding us. That is most important. We can and shall help him. We shall point out certain Health Secrets which should not be "secrets" at all, but common knowledge to Earthlings. At the Lifetronic Healing Center on Venus, we give out these and other teachings freely so that all Venusians learn how to work with Nature's upbuilding measures, from infancy on.

"In Jim Lindy's case, he must first intensify his desire to be well. Then he himself must send forth his desire directly to us and we shall give him a sign of our recognition, and illumine his inner consciousness from time to time. This we shall do by a series of **DREAM CONTACTS** in which Jim will sense our positive presence, but not see us. These contacts will be made by us while Jim is sleeping soundly at night. He will at those times experience unusually vivid dreams, each containing a vitally important message for him. Later on, after Jim has made real progress in regaining his health, and has raised his vibrations into a finer and higher frequency, we can then permit him to see us and work with us consciously."

THIS SIDE FOR STUDENT NOTES

"You believe then," I said quickly, "that Jim Lindy can be cured so that he will once again be vigorous and healthy?"

"There are no cures," replied Lon-Zara. "Jim's present state of painful illness was created by himself through his own unwise actions in the PAST. We have no control over what has happened in the past, therefore we cannot "cure" its results. Those who claim they can cure disease are charlatans. They are only fooling themselves and those, homiest souls who turn to them in misguided trust and confidence. The simple truth is, humanity does not have to CURE disease. All it needs to do is stop causing it. This is the first great secret of regaining vibrant, joyous health. While it is true that Jim Lindy has no power over his past acts, he does have the power to choose and control his present actions TODAY.

"This is his God-given right and also responsibility. The moment Jim realizes this, he can at once begin to REVERSE the pattern of "disease" that he created in the past, by replacing it with a vital new pattern of HEALTH. In this way, he will be actively building for the future and in due time the marvelous forces of Nature will do their healing work in his body."

"But is not that a terribly slow process?" I inquired. "For it seemed to me that Nature usually requires much time to mend the results of man's common ills and injuries."

"Ordinarily, yes," said Lon-Zara. "Natural forces do work slowly when unaided by the powers residing within each living human being, namely the mental and soul powers. The average person on earth, when ill or injured, thinks he has no control over the healing process. He leaves it entirely in the hands of Nature. Nature, if unobstructed by the unwise actions of the individual or his doctor, then does her good work of restoring health and harmony in the body. Time is essential in Nature's plan, because her laws are automatic and based upon cause and effect, action and reaction. Plant an apple seed and you do not expect a full-grown tree to rise up overnight, loaded with beautiful apples all ready to eat. We must always consider the natural TIME FACTOR and allow for it, when leaving the healing process entirely in Nature's hands.

"Many thousands of years ago, reckoning according to your earth time, the greatest minds of Venus found that the TIME FACTOR in Nature could be so minimized and reduced that we were able to accomplish results in weeks where formerly years were required. Then we progressed to a point where we could do as

THIS SIDE FOR STUDENT NOTES

much in only a few days as we used to do in several weeks. Finally, our greatest "breakthrough" came when we discovered how to COLLAPSE TIME within our own consciousness so that positive results were realized in mere seconds and minutes that previously took many hours and days to achieve.

"At the Lifetronic Healing Center on Venus, we had long studied the simple, marvelous laws of the universe and the forces of Nature. Knowing as we did, that these "natural laws" are designed by the Creator for the good of all life, we did not attempt to change the unchangeable. Instead we did our best to learn those wonderful laws and attune ourselves with them. As we ourselves learned higher truths, we taught them to all the people and showed them how to apply simple methods that brought health and happiness into their lives. To study and apply all that we can discover of our Creator's simple but wonderful principles brings us the greatest of all Joys. Our "Delight" is (as your psalm has it) in the Law of the Lord.

"Our people," continued Lon-Zara, "became aware that health is the physical body1s normal reaction to a normal environment. And a normal environment consists simply of:

1. VITAL AIR

2. VITAL SUNLIGHT

3. VITAL FOOD

4. VITAL WATER

"These are the four supreme essentials for human life. Nature provides these life essentials in a VITAL form, that is, each essential contains a certain amount of positive ELECTRICITY...not the identical electricity that powers your city limits but a finer frequency of the same force which the human body can utilize for the energizing of every living cell. We call this force LIFETRONIC ENERGY, or simply 'LE'.

"When the four life essentials are supplied to your body in a VITAL form, your body reacts to the positive stimulus of 'IE' in its normal, intended way, by functioning harmoniously. This causes you to feel well, energetic and at perfect 'ease'. However, what would happen if you changed the four essentials of your normal environment to:

1. DEAD AIR

2. WEAK SUNLIGHT

THIS SIDE FOR STUDENT NOTES

3. DEAD FOOD

4. DEAD WATER

"My environment would then be abnormal and I would get ill, age rapidly, and die prematurely," I reasoned.

"And do you also see that your physical ills and early death would, under those conditions, be perfectly normal reactions to an abnormal environment?" asked the Venusian.

"Yes," I responded, "As I understand it now from what you have said, both health and disease are normal reactions. In simple terms, HEALTH, PLEASANT REACTIONS OR 'EASE'; whereas DISEASE = UNPLEASANT REACTIONS OR DISEASE." The most important factor in either condition is the quality and quantity of LIFETRONIC ENERGY that is contained in a person's environment. A normal environment produces HEALTH because it provides plenty of 'LE' through vital air, food, sunlight and water. On the other hand, an insufficiency of 'LE' deprives the body of its life power-electricity-and this affects the body adversely."

"Correct," said Lon-Zara. "Now let us see how your friend Jim Lindy has unwittingly interfered with the four life essentials and thereby seriously lowered his intake of 'LE'.

"First, Jim Lindy has been breathing DEAD AIR instead of live, fresh, moving air. Inactive air is like a stagnant pool of water. It contains almost no positive electricity. To build health he must have vital, fresh out-door air. Also, he must form a habit of exercising regularly out of doors so that the activity – will force him to breathe deeply, thus pumping the LIFETRONIC ENERGY to all parts of his body.

"Second, Jim has not fully realized how much his physical body-which is composed of vibrating ATOMS-requires the higher vibratory ATOMIC STIMULUS of the sun's rays. It is possible to live with little or no sunlight but the result is never a happy one for the body craves the 'LE' radiated to all living things from the central sun of this solar system.

"Third, like the great majority of humans on planet earth, Jim Lindy has relied upon cooked food to energize his body. This is a serious error, for it is impossible to get something vital out of something dead. Cooked and processed food is nine-tenths dead, for the 'LE' that was originally in the food has been forced out of it into the atmosphere by the vibratory action of the fire. If one knows how to consciously extract

THIS SIDE FOR STUDENT NOTES

more 'LE' out of the air (via exercise and certain mental techniques) he can 'get by' on cooked food longer than one who neglects to supply his body with 'LE' from those other sources. However, no true adept or master on any planet eats cooked food, for it is contrary to natural law and always has a destructive effect.

"Fourth, Jim has drunk freely of the ordinary reservoir water and of water from mineral springs of the earth. Although this water contains a certain amount of 'LE' derived through contact with sun and air, it also contains quantities of inorganic minerals. These minerals are too low and coarse in vibration to be used by the human body, and although the plant kingdom may thrive on them, the human body deposits them in various organs, bony joints, etc. All these dead minerals irritate the nerves, stiffen the body and bring about the symptoms of old age which now plague your friend Jim."

I realized that live, organic water is obtained by simply eating fresh, juicy fruits. Moreover, I knew that the vast majority of men, women and children on planet Earth do not live in a truly "normal" environment. All of us deprive ourselves, in one or more of the four ways mentioned, of the LIFETRONIC ENERGY we need for positive health. Luckily, some people are able to get enough extra "LE" from one or two of the four sources, to make up in part for its great lack in other sources.

The Venusians undoubtedly had discovered methods of consciously increasing their intake of "LE"...possibly by mind and soul power. Quietly Lon-Zara terminated our mental contact and I fell asleep.

THIS SIDE FOR STUDENT NOTES

THREE RIVERS TO CROSS
Part Three

I awoke early next morning, and eagerly made my way to the guest room to greet Jim Lindy with a cheery "Good morning". To my delight he was already dressed and ready and willing to join me in my regular "morning constitutional" which consists simply of a brisk, one-mile walk before breakfast.

Jim's blue eyes had a sparkle in them that I hadn't seen in years. Although It was apparent that he had not been healed in any magical way while he slept, I sensed that he had been given a sign of hope and illumination from the Space Brothers. as we walked, Jim spoke quietly. His voice was vibrant with an unusual, inner excitement. He said that, during his sleep he had experienced a most remarkable dream. But unlike ordinary nightly dreams, this one was INTENSELY REAL, VIVID and POWERFULLY SOUL MOVING. In this extraordinary dream he saw himself - sick, weak and senile - standing on a sandy shore at the edge of THREE GREAT RIVERS which ran parallel to each other. Puzzled at finding himself standing at this strange spot, he stepped back away from the edge of the water. As he did so, he heard a deeply melodious voice say, "The Elixir of Life awaits you beyond the Third River. Have COURAGE and claim your heritage!"

Reacting positively to the challenge, Jim plunged boldly Into the First River and began to swim to the other side. But...weakened as he was by illness, he found it a severe, hard struggle to cross the River. Refusing to "give in" to his troubles, Jim called forth strength he did not even know he had, and at last managed to reach the other side of the First River. And, instead of feeling worse for the vigorous ordeal, he was astonished to find that he felt much better.

THIS SIDE FOR STUDENT NOTES

Encouraged by his success, he entered the Second River bravely, but the strong undercurrent made him fearful of being pulled under and drowned. His fear Increased until he thought of the Prize beyond the Third River. What was the "Elixir of Life"? What would it do for him if he imbibed that Elixir?

He must know, despite all obstacles. Suddenly new courage and power flowed into him and his fear left him. He redoubled his efforts and with an ease that surprised him, crossed the Second Great River. Now the Third River confronted him. It was by far the deepest, widest, muddiest river of the three. When he entered the river, great quantities of mud and dirt and slime were so stirred up that it became very difficult to see the opposite shore. At times the swimming became actually painful, so that he almost forgot why he was struggling against such powerful odds in his "condition". He thought, Wouldn't it be wiser and easier to go back to the place where I started from and try to find some OTHER WAY to cross this final river?" He was just about to turn back when he heard the same marvelous voice say: "There is no other way. This is your final chance to claim the Prize. Go onward! Go onward!"

And onward Jim went, in spite of "hell and high water", until at last he had overcome the third and final river and stood triumphant on the gleaming white shore at its opposite side. But where was the Elixir of Life? He could not see anything by that name waiting for him. However, he noticed that he was now in a beautiful fruit orchard. In fact it looked very much as he had imagined the Biblical "Garden of Eden" roust have looked. Luscious tropical fruits hung from heavily laden trees all around him. Hungry from his recent physical exertions, Jim gratefully sampled some of the tree-ripened fruit and found it amazingly delicious and wholesome.

In a few moments he had satisfied his natural hunger by eating his fill of the wonderful fruit, and then he received a most astounding and exceedingly pleasant surprise.

In some strange way - beyond his ability to account for—his entire being had undergone a most amazing transformation. Looking at his body, he noted with a thrill of utter amazement that it had become youthful, strong and handsome. Every cell of his being now radiated health whereas before it seemed to him that the "Grim Reaper" was very close by and was only waiting for a chance to make one last swing with his deadly sickle. What a thrill to realize that he had outwitted that "old boy", and that health, youth and joy were once more living realities to him. Then the dream—for it WAS a dream—faded, and Jim awakened from his sleep.

THIS SIDE FOR STUDENT NOTES

Eagerly he rushed to a mirror to see if by some "magic" means the wonderful dream had come true. So real had the experience been to Jim, it seemed that surely it must have happened. But as he gazed into the mirror he saw at once that no magic had taken place...at least any that was evident immediately to the eyes. His body was still sickly looking, prematurely old and lacking in vital strength. An unusually vibrant sparkle, however, shone strongly in his blue eyes, as if he had contacted living forces that could quite easily—if they so willed — "transform" him into the healthy, happy, individual he longed to be. This, briefly, was the inspiring first DREAM-CONTACT as Jim related it to roe while we walked.

"A truly wonderful experience," I remarked. "No doubt it has an inner meaning that will shed much light on your health problem. Let us gradually try to comprehend it to the fullest."

By the time we had reached the apartment we had worked up quite an appetite for breakfast. Already Jim seemed to be feeling better, and it delighted my soul to see him sit down at the breakfast table with roe and eat his share of the paradisiacal foods Lenore placed before us. These consisted of fresh, delicious organic fruits sliced into a generous sized bowl, and topped with sunflower seeds, almond-nut cream and a sprig of mint-leaf. All items in our diet are always entirely uncooked, unprocessed and completely wholesome. Lenore is very careful about this. After one lives on natural, uncooked foods for a time, the age-old cultivated taste for unnatural, cooked foods fades away. You can tell at once that the "Life Vibration" is missing in the foods that have been subjected to fire.

After breakfast Jim busied himself by writing some important letters to his family and friends in Washington State. For this task, I let him use my "den" where he could type the letters on my typewriter without being disturbed by anyone.

While he was occupied constructively, I went into my library room to catch up on some serious reading. My library is somewhat unique in that it contains several thousand books chiefly of an occult or mystical nature. My collection of "Flying Saucer", "Space Flight", and "Interplanetary" books is amazingly complete and of course, highly treasured.

I began searching through the shelves for something on the subject of "health, thinking that I might find an especially enlightening book I could recommend to Jim. However, I was disappointed to find that the books, while excellent, contained nothing really new or revolutionary in them. The general conclusions seemed to be that the

THIS SIDE FOR STUDENT NOTES

why and wherefore of vigorous health are still a deep mystery to science. When human beings get sick, they are being "attacked" by ferocious little germs that just can't stand to see anybody stay healthy and happy. The usual treatment suggested by most of the well-intentioned (?) authorities includes Vitamin Supplements, Medicines, Laxatives and other nostrums too numerous and complex to mention. Surely the Space Brothers had a simpler and more certain approach to health. Surely they had better solutions.

Suddenly I felt that peculiar sense of peace, harmony and timelessness. Again Lon-Zara was contacting me telepathically, or rather, by Telethot communication. I could hardly wait to ask him about the THREE RIVERS that Jim Lindy had "crossed" in his dream last night. What did those rivers signify?

"The first River," Lon-Zara explained, "represents the basic, primary NEED to CLEANSE the mind of negative thoughts, false traditional or "race thinking", and the error of reasoning from false or wrong premises. As long as Jim Lindy clings to the useless mental habit of worshipping FALSE GODS he will remain confused and sick. False gods 'are those ideas, beliefs and practices based upon human ignorance, willful deceit or mystifying complexity. They Invariably BLOCK the constructive healing power of the natural LIFE FORCES. This is why most methods of healing human ills on your planet are so ineffective. Many of them are ridiculous. Some are actually DESTRUCTIVE. Why? Because they ignore the divine intelligence or GOD-POWER within the individual and interfere with its natural activity which is always working toward GOOD.

"To cleanse the mind, let Jim make a serious effort to cast out all former worship of false authority, and to anchor his life to the GOD CENTER (Life, Love & Intelligence) within himself. New light and understanding will then flow into his mind for he will then be 'centered1 rightly. 'Working from that true center, he will then be able to get into harmony with ALL NATURAL LAWS...and he will find them to be simple, reliable and positive.

"Simplicity in all things, is the keynote of Nature, and therefore it is also the keynote of the Wise Ones. On Venus we have a saying; 'TRUTH IS SIMPLE, FALSITY IS EVER COMPLEX'. A thing is not true merely because it has a great superstructure of complexity. Rather, a thing is true if it is based upon a principle or law that actually exists in Nature. Jim believes that because disease appears so mysterious to him, its remedy must also be mysterious. This is not so. He must awaken to the truth that HEALTH IS MAN'S NORMAL AND NATURAL CONDITION. It is simply the natural result of living in a normal environment of air, sun, food and water. However, even a

THIS SIDE FOR STUDENT NOTES

normal environment will not fully restore Jim's health if his mind is not working in tune with Nature.

"Negative, false beliefs are powerless to build. They only confuse, confound and destroy main's health and harmony. For a healthy, sane, simple and satisfying life - Jim must CAST THEM OUT by seeing them for what they really are. Then, new and positive ideas based upon true, natural principles, can work for him without hindrance from the old ideas. This is the meaning of the First River, which all humans must cross.

"The Second River", continued my Venusian Teacher, "represents the great NEED to cleanse the emotional or desire nature of Jim Lindy. As long as his soul remains asleep to the vital importance of the positive LOVE emotion as the universal harmonizing, stabilizing, protecting influence, just so long will his desires be of a negative and harmful kind. Desires are based upon the fulfilling of physical sensations. Such age-old racial habits as eating highly spiced, cooked food, particularly animal flesh, strong drink and other destructive influences which are not man's natural foods at all, came about and lingered on through the centuries, simply because of this urge to experience physical sensation. His appetites and sensations resulting from the use of these unnatural foods have created negative emotional desires in the majority of Earthlings and now we see in Jim Lindy, a modem example of this sad error. Negative desires act to crowd out the higher LOVE nature in man, thereby causing him to suffer all the foolishly negative emotions of fear, hate, Jealousy, revenge, resentment, etc. These are all BARRIERS to perfect HEALTH.

"By developing a higher LOVE NATURE that desires the well-being and happiness of all living creatures, Jim will come to see that the life of our Younger Brothers, the animals, is just as important to THEM as our life is to US. lie will then cease eating them. His whole desire nature will be uplifted and the old appetites will fall away automatically. He will enter into a deeper harmony with all the forces of LIFE. This is the basic meaning of the Second River that Jim must cross.

"The Third River signified the GREAT NEED TO CLEANSE ALL THE CELLS of the physical body, as well as the ATOMS of which those cells are composed. A clean foundation is necessary if Jim is to rebuild for himself a virile, positive NEW AGE BODY."

"How may this atom-cleansing be accomplished?" I asked.

THIS SIDE FOR STUDENT NOTES

"A CLEANSING FAST of 1 day will begin the good work." replied Lon-Zara. "A short fast is of great value as it allows the body to begin eliminating its burden of waste. No food of any kind is to be taken during this short fast. Pure distilled water, however, to which the Juice of fresh lemon or orange is added in the proportion of 1% Juice to 99% water, should be taken freely, a glassful every one or two hours as desired.

"On the second day, diluted fresh fruit Juice (lemon, orange or grapefruit) may be taken in proportion of 50% juice to 50% water, a glassful every hour during the day.

"On the 3rd day, a CLEANSING FEAST of fresh fruits is indicated. Jim Lindy may eat abundantly his choice of any of the following fresh, Juicy fruits:

Apples, peaches, pears, papaya, grapes, plums, apricots, nectarines, mangos, persimmons, cherries, fresh figs, sapotes, oranges, Texas-Pink grapefruit, melon (all kinds), tomatoes. (Yes, tomatoes are a fruit.)

"No other foods are to be eaten during this 3rd day of cleansing. Fresh fruits are the most eliminating of all foods and have the highest electrical vibration. They should be eaten in their natural, unfired, tree-ripened state. (NOTE: Avoid using fruits sprayed by chemical poisons. Non-sprayed, 100% organic fresh fruits are now sold in most stores.)

"Only one kind of fruit is eaten at a meal. However, as much of that fruit may be eaten as is desired. Meals may be spaced three hours apart, and a different kind of fruit eaten at each meal so that variety is obtained in this manner.

"The electrical energy of Life is transmitted by Nature to all living plants, and is very abundant in Juicy, ripe fruit. All fruit is, in its natural, uncooked state, filled with vital, highly electrified ORGANIC WATER. Life always attracts MORE life. Death attracts more death. Earthlings such as Jim Lindy who partake freely of delicious, Juicy fruits are in no way adding further impurities to obstruct the body. Rather they are bathing their cells internally with a CLEANSING ORGANIC WATER. Old age deposits cannot withstand this living water. It is far superior to ordinary drinking water, which, being inorganic and harmful, is never used by the men and women of Venus for drinking purposes.

"On the 4th day Jim Lindy may return to his complete New Age Diet of fruits, nuts, sprouts and vegetables. By practicing this CLEANSING REGIME once each

THIS SIDE FOR STUDENT NOTES

month, Jim will be amazed and delighted by the rapidity of his physical improvement."

"Is there any specific name to Jim's disease?" I ventured to ask at this point in our communication.

"On Venus we recognize only ONE basic cause of human Dis-Ease ," replied Lon-Zara, "and that is LIFETRONIC DEPLETION. The electric power in the human body is run down. This is usually due to man's foolish attempt to change his normal environment into an abnormal one. Man does this by refusing to exercise, avoiding the sunlight, cooking his food, eating foods for which his alimentary tract is not adapted, and thinking negatively. All of these practices are completely contrary to Nature's rules of harmony. Hence, they continually CLOG the body with Impurities. This prevents a NORMAL INTAKE of enough 'LE' to vitalize and regenerate the bodily cells.

"Jim's ailments are in no sense mysterious to us. He has simply CONGESTED and abused the digestive and eliminative organs of his body through negative thinking, wrong food and harmful emotions. His stomach, liver and intestines have suffered greatly. As a result, his whole electronic body is now unbalanced. Moreover, his 'over-treatments' in the wrong direction have not only confused his mind, but filled his system with drug poisons which have to be eliminated from Jim's body before vibrant health is possible.

"All three phases of being, Body, Mind and Soul, must be cleansed of obstructing wastes so that the Spirit of Jim's entire and perfect self can function freely and Joyously. It is then that his true Higher Purpose in life will be revealed to him. To succeed in his present desire to regain his health, it is important for Jim to believe in a Power greater than he is. A Power in which he can place implicit faith. All sick individuals will get well faster by recognizing a basic law of GOOD and GROWTH that is always working for their ultimate perfection. There is ONE POWER in the universe and it is good. Man can either USE it or BLOCK it; but he cannot change it.

"At the appropriate point we can tremendously accelerate Jim's progress toward health. However, he himself must take these first THREE STEPS voluntarily and without our personal aid. He must 'cross the Three Rivers' courageously. Once he does this-and many have crossed before him - he shall know the truth for himself...that it is much EASIER to be healthy, strong and youthful than to be sick, weak and old! Moreover, he will realize that germs and viruses are not the primary causes of Dis-

THIS SIDE FOR STUDENT NOTES

Ease as he has been misled to believe. Instead, they are merely SCAVENGERS whose natural function is to reduce dead cells back to their original chemical elements."

I remembered having once seen buzzards around a dead cow in a pasture, and asked Lon-Zara if the germs came to clean up an ailing body much as buzzards fed on dead tissue. He agreed it was so.

"Germs are always 'secondary agents' in Dis-Ease and never the primary cause. Of course, germs do make a person feel exceedingly miserable. But even so, they are serving a good purpose in breaking down the mucus and phlegm in the body so that it can be excreted more easily. Once you know that buzzards are never attracted to living cells (live tissue) but only to dead carrion, you lose all fear of germs forever. If the body is kept clean inside as well as out, by NOT PUTTING DEAD CELLS INTO THE BODY VIA DEAD FOOD, the boldest germ will refuse to have the slightest thing to do with such a body. The elimination regime helps clean the body inside. Then the REAL CAUSE of bodily ills - LIFETRONIC DEPLETION - is avoided, because there is NO CONGESTED WASTE in the system to block the inflow of the vital life force."

I had one more question.

"The Prize, the Elixir of Life, what is it?"

Lon-Zara paused a long moment before replying. I sensed that what he was about to divulge was highly important.

"VRIL-POWER," the master said, "the most subtle, and when skillfully wielded, the most powerful of all forces. Of this you will learn more in a later communication. Preparation to be worthy of the prize, is the most immediate concern."

THIS SIDE FOR STUDENT NOTES

HOW TO GIVE UP YOUR ILLS

Part Four

DURING lunch, I told Jim Lindy about the contact with my space friend, Lon-Zara. I explained, as best I could from memory, the important significance of Jim's remarkable dream about the "Three Rivers". Far from being skeptical concerning the marvelous and practical information revealed by the Venusian, Jim was intensely pleased and enthusiastic.

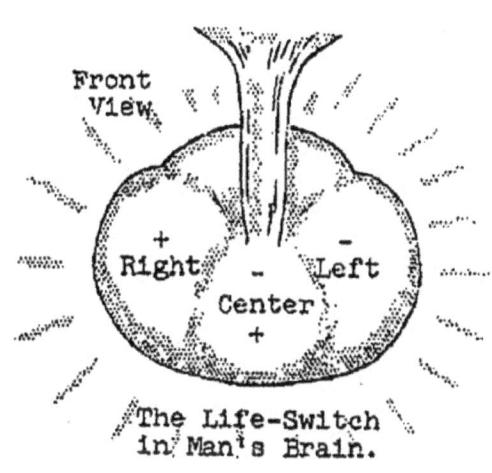

The Life-Switch in Man's Brain.

"Wonderful", he exclaimed earnestly. "Thanks to Lon-Zara and you, Michael, I am at last beginning to see my way out of the health problems that have bewildered me for so long. As you have pointed out, Dis-Ease is really no deep, dark mystery as I have been taught to believe since I was a child. It is just a case of excessive waste matter in my body due to the constant eating of "dead food". I see now that it is unreasonable to expect LIFE to manifest abundantly in my body unless I abandon 'death habits' of eating, thinking and feeling, and start at once to acquire 'life habits' which CLEANSE and vitalize my body, mind and soul. I did this symbolically in my dream by crossing the three rivers. Now I must go a step further and apply these purification measures in my personal life right now. You know I want to get rid of my ills..."(at this point Jim enumerated a long list of afflictions that he was troubled with, including liver disorder, stomach pains, gall bladder pains, swollen joints, bowel stasis, etc, etc.)

It sounded pretty hopeless. All those physical troubles...maybe Jim's predicament was more serious than I had imagined. He needed help, but it must be of

THIS SIDE FOR STUDENT NOTES

the right kind. Already the Space People had given us much practical guidance, but I sensed that the next hurdle would be more challenging. It is one thing to dream about doing something, and quite another thing to accomplish it in the conscious, waking state.

I encouraged Jim to keep his thoughts and feelings cheerful and optimistic regarding his health. A gentle reminder that the Space People were "on his side", and that Lon-Zara himself was one of the most advanced healers in the Lifetronic Healing Center on Venus, set his mind at ease. He strolled out to the back garden for his usual routine "sun bath". As I watched him settle back in the comfortable lawn chair and close his eyes for a brief nap in the warm sun, I couldn't help thinking, "There is a physical wreck if ever I saw one."

It will certainly take some 'magic1 beyond my knowledge to get him back on the positive side of REAL HEALTH again. But in spite of his predicament, he is a good soul and a brave one. I hope he makes it.

Suddenly I became aware of Lon-Zara's mental signal, and again we were in telepathic communication. The contact lasted several minutes, the gist of it being as follows:

"Jim Lindy should begin at once on his purification Program under the personal care and instructions of a certain 'Doctor C' who lives in Los Angeles." (Dr. C is an earth brother whom I have known for a number of years. Not only is Dr. C a believer in the existence of the Space people, he is also in frequent communication with them and cooperates fully with their requests which are for the upliftment of humanity.)

I was advised by Lon-Zara that the wonderful method of Lifetronic Healing used on Venus, is known and utilized on all of the higher planets beyond the earth. However, only a rare few mortals on earth have increased their soul-awareness to the point where they are conscious of the principle whereby the method works, Dr. C is held in highest esteem by the Space People. He is, I believe, the only human on earth that has developed himself to that high degree of proficiency whereby he is able to consciously project LIFETRONIC ENERGY into other living human bodies, with the same remarkable effectiveness as the Venusian Healers. I was also given to understand that my good friend Dr. C was in his past life incarnated on the planet Venus. There he learned the God-principle of LIFETRONIC HEALING, and dedicated himself to the avowed task of helping Earth's suffering humanity. By his own conscious choice, Dr. C

THIS SIDE FOR STUDENT NOTES

was reincarnated on earth. During his present earth-life, Dr. C. recognized (remembered or knew again) the Lifetronic Healing principle.

Lon-Zara explained to me that, while It was entirely possible for Jim Lindy to apply many of the health instructions at my home, it was wiser for us to do so under the guidance of an earth brother such as Dr. C. Inasmuch as Dr. C is a qualified practicing D.C., his services in Jim Lindy's case would prove most valuable. I was assured that Dr. C would bring great blessings to Jim.

That evening, I took Jim to see the amazing Dr. C. His home, happily, was located not far distant from my own, and a brief auto ride soon brought us to his door. Before I could ring the doorbell to announce our arrival, the door swung open and with a pleasant smile the doctor himself stood in the entrance; his hands outstretched to greet us.

"Come In," he said pleasantly, "I've been expecting you."

He directed Jim Lindy and me into the adjusting room, where we talked for a few moments about Jim's condition, the recent contacts by Telethot with the Space People, and their instructions. Dr. C looked calmly into my eyes while he spoke, and I realized that he was already aware of the events which had transpired since my friend Jim Lindy had made his unexpected appearance.

The doctor is a tall, well proportioned man in his seventies. He has large blue eyes that sparkle at times with a sudden brilliance and depth almost as if they were blue diamonds. This seems to be a positive characteristic of all spiritually advanced beings, for their soul is charged with powerful life spirit which radiates out through the eyes. In appearance, Dr. C is noble in bearing. His every gesture is confidence-inspiring, but it is not the kind of useless confidence based on man-made concoctions and poison drugs. Instead, it is a confidence built upon the rock of God-principle which is eternally true and certain in its workings.

The first thing Dr. C did was to check the physical alignment of Jim's body. Most people, the doctor has found, are very much out of alignment physically. One side of their body is usually shorter or longer than the other side. That is why, when you look at photographs of some people you will notice that one eye is often much lower than the other, or one shoulder is higher than the other.

What is the reason for this? Electrical imbalance, explains Dr. C. The human body directs its Lifetronic Energy from a central switch in the brain, known as the

THIS SIDE FOR STUDENT NOTES

"Life Switch." This Switch is actually the Pituitary Gland located in the approximate center of the head about two-inches back of the eyes. It has three lobes, known as left, center, and right lobes.

Negative thinking, or any emotional feeling which is of a destructive or negative nature, cramps the Life Switch by contracting it so that it is low and twisting. If it should become contracted in the left lobe, the entire left side of the physical body at once contracts or shortens...sometimes by several inches. This would make the left arm and leg noticeably shorter than the right arm or leg. The same effect occurs if you cramp the right lobe of the Pituitary Gland, the contracting effect being on the right side of the body Instead of the left. As Dr. C pointed out, Jim Lindy was electrically "short-circuited" on the right side of his body. When the Life-Switch is high, or the individual is "on center", then the right and the left sides of the body are perfectly even.

The terra "Short-Circuit", as you know, is used when dealing with electrical circuits. If a current of electricity is unable to get through a circuit or "path" due to some obstruction, the current is said to be "shorted out". In Jim's case, there was definitely not enough LIFETRONIC ENERGY getting through the right lobe of his Life Switch. Without sufficient electrical power to vitalize and animate the right side of his body, all of the organs and glands located on that side-liver, gall-bladder, etc., were being deprived of health and well-being. To confirm this fact, Jim's body proved to be much shorter on the right side...the right leg and arm being two full inches shorter than the left. His right eye was noticeably lower than the left eye.

"I shall now project an impulse of Lifetronic Power from my own brain into the right side of Jim's Life Switch," said Dr. C, "and you can observe the change immediately."

Jim was, at this moment, standing up flat against the wall of the room, facing outward from the wall. I kept my eye on him so that I could detect any perceptible improvement. I did not have to wait long. Dr. C simply closed his eyes for a second and the "miracle" happened. Jim's entire body, right and left sides, instantaneously came into perfect balance and alignment. Both eyes were perfectly level and limbs equal.

Amazing? To observers like Jim and I, yes. But to the good doctor and the Venusians it is an everyday occurrence and in complete harmony with God's law of healing. According to Dr. C, the strong electric Impulse from his own brain center had flashed instantly through space and into the Life Switch of Jim Lindy where it RAISED

THIS SIDE FOR STUDENT NOTES

that Switch physically – or shall we say magnetically – so that it no longer was cramped. When this was done, Lifetronic Energy automatically flowed into and through the Switch, putting the body into true balance.

Jim Lindy was deeply impressed, for he had looked into a mirror Just before Dr. C raised his Life Switch, and he had seen for himself that one eye was much lower than the other.

Now they were absolutely level and the doctor hadn't so much as laid a hand on his head to "adjust" it in any way. Here indeed was magic. Yet it was high magic, white magic, directed by the healer in a wise manner to overcome man's Dis-Ease .

"Am I healed of my ills?" Jim asked excitedly.

"Your Life-Switch is now raised high," said the doctor.

We've turned on the Lifetronic current for you, just like we would turn on the Light switch in our house so the electric lights can shine. This is the most important thing to do in all healing. Some healers do it accidentally and the patient gets well; but they do not understand what the principle is that caused the healing to take place. We have found out how to use the principle consciously, and direct It anywhere in the universe by our thought and will. This Is the same principle that Jesus used when he raised Lazarus from the tomb... he projected Life Electricity into the brain of Lazarus and "turned on" his Life Switch I But now you' asked if you are fully healed of your ills?

"I have helped your body restore its strength and wellbeing by opening the channels for Life to pour into you," continued Dr. C, "and you will now get well and strong. But you should know that health is not only a matter of getting your physical body aligned and balanced. The mind must also be made to work for your health and upbuilding. If you fail to heed this suggestion, and continue to think about all the afflictions that you have suffered from, the Life Switch will again contract and reduce your supply of vital power.

"Thinking about your disease and yet, hoping for something or somebody to bring you health, is like trying to back out toward health. You keep seeing the affliction so clearly that all you can possibly realize is more of that affliction. You are giving the innate mind within you a perfect picture of disease and that is what it produces for you. What to do? Reverse attention! Head out toward the HEALTH you want, don't try to back out toward it? Get your thoughts fixed on HEALTH and target the "disease

THIS SIDE FOR STUDENT NOTES

images" that will give your subconscious mind a new directive to work on, and you will be surprised at the results. Just remember not to "rescind" the order. You want health and NOT Dis-Ease!"

"You mean I am to give up my ills mentally?" Jim inquired. He was beginning to grasp the importance of the idea.

"Exactly. Let go of your ills mentally first. Mind always tends to move matter. Make your mind motivate you into healthful activities, thoughts and positive feelings. Otherwise the healing we have done for you will not be permanent, and Nature will again penalize you with pain. Health really means LIFE in harmonious BALANCE. Anything that cuts off Lifetronic power from your body, mind or soul is NEGATIVE for you. Why? Because it turns off your Life Switch little by little. When the Switch turns too far LIFE can't get into your body via the brain...the body then dies.

"All diseases man is heir to will stop and automatically heal themselves the moment he stops causing those ills by negative habits, and begins to get MORE of the electrical or LIFE Energy into the mind, body and soul. When this is done, then the sick individual becomes well, happy and strong."

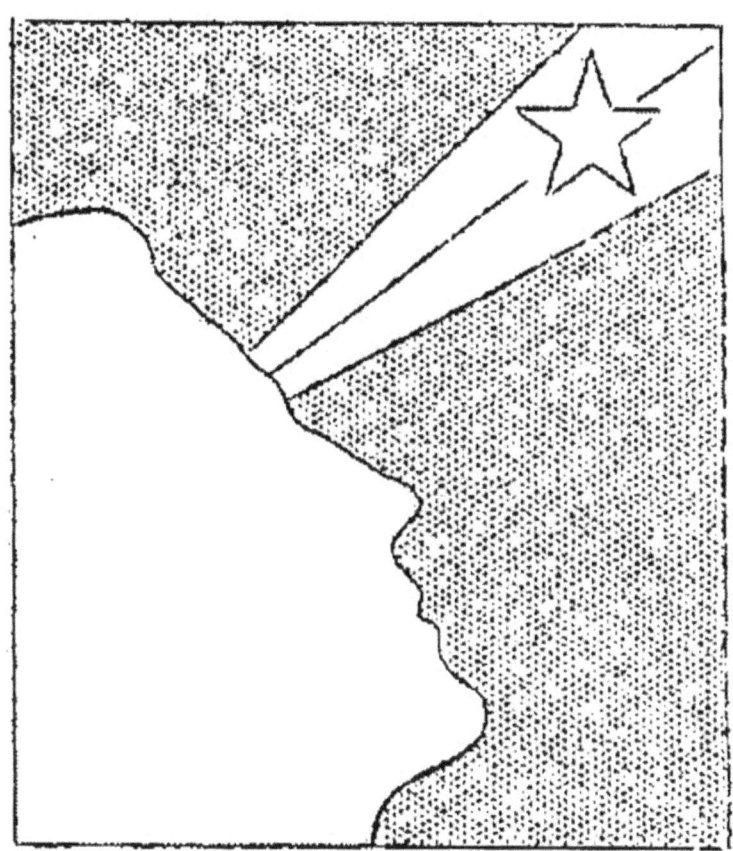

THIS SIDE FOR STUDENT NOTES

THE MAGICAL "LIFETRONS"
Part Five

A month had passed since I first introduced Jim Lindy to the remarkable Dr, C. During this time we kept in close touch with the healer as well as with the Space People. Once or twice a week I took Jim over to the doctor1 s house for a physical, mental and spiritual "recharging", and the good effects were becoming apparent. He was rapidly growing out of his weak and sickly condition. I too, was paying more attention to LIFE than I ever did before, with the happy result that my own body was generating a new health and strength far beyond my expectations.

Any student who has followed our adventure this far must be getting impatient to know more about the wonderful man I call Dr. C. This man is not, as some might suppose, a mere figment of imagination. He is a real, living, breathing, human being the same as you and I. But there is one difference. He recognizes the mighty fact that electric and magnetic currents flow through and interpenetrate all space. These potent forces consist of simple, basic units called LIFETRONS.

A LIFETRON, according to Dr. C., is a Life Electron...a unit of electrical force, energy and power that is akin to SPIRIT itself, for it has an extremely high vibration and is the generator of Life in all living creatures. Most wonderful to know, these Lifetrons fill all space. You and I live in a "sea of Lifetrons". They are all around us as well as within us. The Venusians have learned this countless centuries ago. That is why they say that man cannot die, he is immortal, for Life is everywhere in space, ever sustaining the soul of man.

Of course, it is true that the physical body of man does decay and die, for we see the fact' of physical death in every newspaper we happen to glance through. This sad state of affairs is not due to any desire on the part of God that human beings should

THIS SIDE FOR STUDENT NOTES

lose their physical forms just when they ought to be expressing themselves most creatively in the very prime of life. Man himself shortens his life. How? Simply by getting in tune with Death rather than Life. You see, Life is never static or still. Instead, it is dynamic and moving because it is electrical in essence, and like the current in any dynamo, is constantly "on the go". Proof of this is found in the fact that if you grab hold of an electric wire from that dynamo you get a shock, and instantly.

Life electricity is like that. However, as Dr. C points out, man-made electricity bears little resemblance to the Life Electricity (Lifetronic Power) that God in His infinite wisdom created. The vibratory rate of man-made electricity is too coarse and crude to give life to a living creature. It kills instead of enlivening. But Lifetronic Power flows into and through all living beings, in a never-ending stream of revivifying power which protects and regenerates all that is alive.

You, no matter how poor or sick or miserable you may be, are living in the midst of Divine Forces which can generate a new health and strength in YOUR BODY, weave PROSPERITY and success into your destiny and make your whole life divine and harmonious. The magical "Lifetrons" all around you are overflowing with vitality and health, and the more you study them the closer your mind will get to the Fountain of Life, which will renew your physical body beyond any doubt.

How then, does humanity get out of tune with Life and in tune with Death? For the answer to this question I went again to see my dear friend Dr. C. Jim accompanied me as usual and we both seated ourselves in his comfortable living room. We knew that what he was about to say would be of priceless value not only to us but to the world. As he spoke, in reply to my query, there was a tremendous simplicity, a quietness and dignity about the man. His words seemed to spring from his soul and not from his intellect, and there was complete lack of mere personal ego in his words.

"Mankind thinks, but does not recognize LIFE as a positive reality." He said. "All of us are pretty much aware of the power of thought. The marvelous psychology movements we have seen in recent years have seen to that. But we as yet are blissfully asleep to the reality of LIFETRONIC POWER which is the actual spiritual energy, electricity if you will, that makes the human body live and move and breathe."

"Is that why people look for health in a bottle?" I asked.

"Yes. People are looking for cures in every direction. Medicine in bottles is only one of thousands of different ways by which sick men and women hope to recover their lost health. The reason they usually get worse instead of better, is because they

THIS SIDE FOR STUDENT NOTES

have not become aware of a basic truth of Life, which is: (to express it quite simply) ANYTHING THAT DOES NOT HAVE THE VIBRATIONS OF LIFE IN IT, HAS ABSOLUTELY NO POWER TO INCREASE LIFE IN ANY LIVING CREATURE.

"The reason this is true is because a lower vibration is unable to stimulate or "quicken" a higher vibration. An inorganic mineral for example, HAS SO FEW lifetrons in it that neither animals nor humans can obtain vital energy from such material. Only that which is living and organic is able to nourish and revitalize living creatures."

"Can you explain more fully what you mean by that?"

"Yes and very simply. LIFE and ONLY LIFE can heal a sick body, regardless of the name of its DIS-EASE . And what is Life, essentially? Gods universal SPIRIT or POWER. This is what the ancient Hermetists (students of Hermes Trismegistus in Egypt) termed the ONE POWER that runs the universe. I like to think of it as SPIRITUAL ELECTRICITY.

"When human beings get sick, they call for a doctor. And what does the doctor do? Usually very little that is of real value, for his real Job is to aid Nature when necessary, in removing waste obstructions from the physical body. Those obstructions consist simply of the body's cell excretions, retained food wastes in the bowel's, and excessive mucus. If these material wastes are not eliminated regularly and promptly, they poison the entire system. A wise doctor, therefore, sees that these poisons are eliminated naturally from the body so that LIFE or SPIRITUAL ELECTRICITY can flow into and through the organism more abundantly. The body is then able to restore its electronic balance and return to a natural condition of health or harmony or EASE."

"Then it is LIFE and not the doctor, who does the healing?" I Inquired.

He paused for a second, and then replied:

"Life, or the animating POWER in nature, heals. That is why the true and ancient meaning of the word 'doctor' is actually 'teacher1. A wise and honest doctor can help his patients most by teaching them how to contact more of the LIFETRONIC POWER that fills the universe, and permeates all space. Lifetrons make people well. Lifetrons regenerate and vitalize broken-down bodies. Get more Lifetrons into your body and you automatically become vibrantly well. You'll never be sick as long as you're well. Sickness is something you DON'T have. It's the LACK of HEALTH. So the

THIS SIDE FOR STUDENT NOTES

idea is to become so filled with radiant LIFE that you manifest positive, glowing HEALTH. After all, that is your natural condition. And the only way to know for sure that you are HEALTHY and in tune with LIFE is to know that you HAVE these Lifetrons flowing through you abundantly and freely without obstruction, for then you feel most vital and alive. You should, then, know all you can about them."

Jim and I had both been listening very carefully to everything Dr. C had told us so far. Now we sensed that the SECRET we had been watching for was about to be revealed, and we didn't want to miss a single word.

"The more advanced Space People such as the Venusians," said Dr. C, "know all about the Lifetrons and how to use them in the most direct and positive way. They understand clearly that these potent electric forces of Life animate all the live, vital creations of nature on all planets. Most important, they realize that these divine forces of SPIRIT are obedient to the mind of man, ready to operate powerfully everything for man's good...IF he will but recognize his God-given dominion and direct Life Electricity in harmony with the original purpose and plan of the Creator of All."

"Then it is possible and practical for a Select Few of Earth's humanity to learn how to direct and control the universal Lifetrons by intelligent thought-force?" Jim questioned.

"Truly." The doctor's expression was most earnest. "My own body and the actual demonstrations I make of this healing principle, are living evidence of the truth of it. I use it daily to overcome the effects of Dis-Ease in my patients. When you know how to work it...and you can gain this KNOWLEDGE if you desire it...you will experience one seeming MIRACLE after another each time you apply it. People are brought into my house blind, deaf, suffering from strokes, heart disorders, and countless other symptoms of Lifetronic Depletion. The blind are made to see, the deaf to hear, and so forth. But do not misunderstand. Not everyone is intended by the Wise Creator to be a healer or others. Only, as you say, a select few individuals are evolved enough in mind, body and soul to be entrusted with such potent knowledge.

"Those Spiritually advanced persons on earth, who have a strong desire to help their suffering fellow men by means of the healing Lifetrons, are gradually enlightened by the Space people as to the proper use and development of LIFETRONIC HEALING POWER. At the right time, when they are capable of directing this power rightly, they are shown how to mentally project LIFE ELECTRICITY from their own higher brain centers into the bodies of sick and despairing individuals who desperately need that

THIS SIDE FOR STUDENT NOTES

influx of DYNAMIC LIFE. In this manner, a select few on this earth will become healers. That is, channels for the HEALING POWER It was in this very same way that I first acquired the healing power and through the constant use of it I have found that it has increased in potency a thousand fold!"

At this point a number of patients entered Dr. C's office for treatment, and with the consent of these other patients we were permitted to watch the healing power in action. As he had done with Jim and myself, Dr. C first raised the Life Switch in each ailing individual. Then, by mental control, he poured powerful streams or waves of Lifetrons into their bodies, realigning them electrically so that immediately a more positive degree of vitality manifested physically.

After the treatments had been given, and the patients had departed thoroughly filled with new zest for living, we continued our important conversation with Dr. C. Again the doctor reminded us that it was LIFETRONIC POWER that did the healing, and not merely his "positive thought". Behind our thoughts is intelligence. The role of intelligence is that of a DIRECTOR. It can of itself accomplish nothing. But the moment it links up with POWER then anything Is possible. We had seen proof of that beyond any question of doubt.

The remainder of our conversation dealt specifically with the magical lifetrons and their control by man. Here, briefly, is the gist of our fascinating discussion:

Lifetrons, under the mental direction of a sincere and dedicated soul, man or woman, can relieve all manner of human ills and Injuries. The greater your awareness of lifetrons is, the more of them you will be able to control and "channel" through your own Lifetronic Brain Switch (Pituitary Gland). Low voltage of healing power is due to a small volume of lifetrons being utilized by the healer. High voltage of healing power means that a very large volume of lifetrons are being directed by the healer. Quite naturally, a Lifetronic Healer is never content to merely manifest "low voltage" healing power, for the higher the voltage the more dynamic and instantaneous is the healing.

Venusian healers, and their earth brother Dr. C, are able, because of faithful, diligent practice to sustain an extremely high potency and quantity of "LE" in their physical and etheric bodies. Because they have a knowledge of this great living force and how to apply it, they are able to perform great marvels of healing as well as other feats too numerous to mention lest we go far afield of our subject. The simple fact is, LIFETRONIC ENERGY in all its various rates of vibration or "frequencies", guided by intelligent thought, is the one basic power that runs the whole universe. It is thru the

THIS SIDE FOR STUDENT NOTES

brain via the "Life Switch" that the life force enters the physical body, and is thence distributed to all the cells. In fact, that Life Switch, the Pituitary Gland, is the original basis from which our physical bodies started (it is here that the "seed-pattern" of a human embryo begins to unfold first), and it is the primary or central "control switch" for the Vital Force or Human Electricity that gives LIFE, to each one of us.

"The power flowing through the Life-Switch into all parts of the body, we call the "Life Current". Dynamic physical health depends upon how well we keep the Life Current moving through the body. If we keep the Current active and positive our health increases and we have the awareness of more positive Life in us.

"What causes DIS-EASE? The blockage of this life current at any point in our electronic bodies. With blockage we always have PAIN for the electricity "hacks up" at that point. Blockage can be physical, mental or emotional in mature. Let's start with the physical. A food, for example, that has been subjected to the heat of FIRE (or altered chemically by commercial processing methods) has lost about 90% of its affinity for Lifetrons. LIFETRONS ARE ALWAYS REPELLED BY FIRE!

Without Lifetrons abundantly supplied by natural, unfired foods, the human body finds great difficulty manufacturing sufficient Life Current for POSITIVE HEALTH. Moreover, the residues from unwholesome foods do not have enough Lifetronic energy in them to stimulate natural peristalsis of the intestines. Result – constipation. Food wastes do not move out of the body rapidly enough and this form of BLOCKAGE not only poisons the body, but cramps and depresses the Pituitary Gland. Result— a considerably WEAKER LIFE CURRENT!

I need not mention in great detail the negative effect of destructive thoughts and feelings. They also quickly depress the Life Switch, and as we have seen, this causes ILLS. According to Dr. C and the Space Masters of Venus, electric force of the right frequency, is the universal power that operates the human body, and gives it life. If the body is out of balance or "sick", electricity can balance it and make it well again. Instant healing—as in the miraculous cures that occur regularly at the religious shrine of Lourdes, in France—is of that nature, ELECTRIC. For electricity is a God-Power. When God-Intelligence guides it, it is omnipotent.

This electric force comes from the SUN of our Solar System, and each one of us is also a SUN. We generate electricity and powerful atomic energy within our physical human bodies much like the great sun in the heavens does. We receive an influx of universal MAGNETISM from that sun, convert it into ELECTRICITY by RESISTING it

THIS SIDE FOR STUDENT NOTES

with our body cells, then we step It up to a frequency we can use best, and send It out into the universe again for the benefit of every being.

I am going to show you how to CONTACT the Lifetrons in a very simple way, so that you can begin to derive real and practical benefits from them just as Dr. C and the Space People do. Bear in mind, this is only the first step for you in the important activity of controlling Lifetrons. Their applications in healing work are well nigh limitless. But let us begin at the beginning so that real understanding will be ours.

First, we'll take a brief look at the tiny but mighty electron, the smallest bit of electricity known. These tiny particles exist everywhere. The air you breathe, the food you eat, the pages you are reading-everything is permeated with electrons. All of them are alike, and each one is only one eighteen-hundredths (1/1848) as big as the tiniest atom. Electrons are actually minute "building blocks" of ENERGY which Nature uses in the construction of atoms.

Because they are negative, electrons REPEL one another. And, quite a number of them are "free". This means that they are not attached to any atom of matter at all. They simply move around In space as free as birds. As long as these free electrons are merely moving around in space, they are of no special use or interest to us. But channel them into the human body by conscious mental direction, and they at once become agents of LIFE with the most marvelous power. Their performance then becomes sheer magic. The Space People call these particles Lifetrons, for once they enter the body they add LIFE to it.

THE TECHNIQUE

Here is the basic method you should use for yourself or for others, to develop your awareness of the Lifetrons and direct them into the physical body. This method does two things, **(a)** It brings a great volume of Lifetrons into your body for the purpose of CLEANING OUT all the old, tired, spent or feeble atoms now in your body, **(b)** It recharges the worn-out (feebly electrified) atoms with a new, fresh supply of Lifetrons from the ocean of space all around you. These new Lifetrons carry into the physical body a strong directive to heal, for they are full of the electricity of LIFE and this LIFE desires perfection.

(1.) Relax yourself in a comfortable chair and close your eyes. Mentally picture yourself resting at the bottom of a great ocean of Lifetrons. Imagine that your

THIS SIDE FOR STUDENT NOTES

body is porous like a sponge, through which vast quantities of sparkling bright electrons can pass, like water through a living sponge. Feel the LOVE quality in those Lifetrons, realize how beautifully they GIVE and RE-GIVE of themselves to vitalize your wondrous physical body and all living bodies. KNOW that these Lifetrons are eagerly awaiting your order to stream into your body, to clean out the old and build in the NEW body cells. In this exercise, image the Lifetrons as being of a radiant light pink, almost white color. See them move in a brilliant .swirl of color when you give them the command. Use a RELAXED WILL. Imaging a pink color will step up your vitality. Use light yellow to step up mental activity.. .light blue if you are overweight.

(2.) Center your attention on your Life Switch, the Pituitary gland, which is located about if inches behind the root of the nose, between the eyes. Relax a moment and breathe quietly and easily. Now lift the muscles of your forehead so that your eyebrows are raised as high as possible, with eyes remaining shut. AS you do this, mentally invite the Lifetrons to pour into your Life-Switch in a great wave. Direct them mentally to CLEAN OUT all the old, sickly cells and depleted electrons from head to toes. Instantly, trillions of fresh Lifetrons—like obedient soldiers—will rush into your brain center and down to your toes and then back up and out through the Life Switch into space again. Let this CLEANSING COMMAND stand "as is" for five minutes. All the while you relax and image the good work that is being done.

(3.) After five minutes of Lifetronic Cleansing, you will find the body has become smaller in size and height due to the elimination of countless numbers of old electrons from the body. (Measure before and after, and note the difference.) Now, after your physical "house" has been swept clean by the new Lifetrons, invite them once again into your body via the Life Switch. This time direct them to mentally FILL the entire body and REPLACE the old ones that have been eliminated. Instantly they will pour into the body again. If you will check your height now you should find it has increased noticeably...showing that much wonderful work has been done. You will also find that when you have completed your Lifetronic Cleaning exercise it has imparted a marvelous new feeling of freedom, ease and poise.

Lifetrons are entirely REAL, not imaginary, units of universal energy. You can use them to build the healthy, glorious new you, the YOU the world now needs and is crying for. This special exercise does not correct your wrong habits of thought or

THIS SIDE FOR STUDENT NOTES

feeling, for only your daily, determined watchfulness can do that; but it can be used effectively to rid the body of accumulations of past thought errors as they are affecting the body now. It also enables you to RE-BALANCE your electronic circuits, thus putting your physical body in tune with the Divine Spark within you, your Higher Self. For your higher good I now urge you to use this technique as Jim and I do, once each day. Seek to know and LOVE the Lifetrons. Become increasingly aware that they exist all about you and your own power to direct them for healing purposes will grow rapidly.

THIS SIDE FOR STUDENT NOTES

POLISHING A LIVING PYRAMID

Part Six

THE following weeks were filled with healthful and constructive activities for both Jim and myself, for I put him to very good use in the garden while I kept busy in my "den". The very marvelous new health knowledge we had received so far was now shaping itself into a most vital instruction course, and even as I made motes of what we'd learned, I sensed that much more health wisdom was soon to be transmitted to us.

Realizing, however, that the Space People never advance new knowledge until the student has mastered that has already been given him, both Jim and I practiced the lifetronic cleansing exercise regularly each day. At first our "awareness" of the Lifetrons in which we all live and move and have our being, was not as keen as it should be. No unusual sensations were felt during our practice. But soon, due to our enthusiasm and persistence, positive results were noticeable by both of us in the form of a pleasant tingle as trillions of tiny "Lifetrons" flashed into our bodies to perform their important services.

A keen, positive awareness of the REALITY of the magical Lifetrons is the main requirement on the part of the sincere student. Merely knowing "intellectually" about the existence of Lifetrons is not enough. That will not accomplish the results. A person can know "all about" the art of swimming and still not be able to swim. But, when one actually enters the water, contacts it physically and finds it will keep him afloat...THEN he or she is AWARE of the water and is able to swim. My impression that additional valuable instruction was soon to be forthcoming proved to be correct. It came in the form of a series of telepathic contacts from Lon-Zara, my beloved Teacher and Master of Lifetronic Healing. These mental contacts or communications occurred with clock-like regularity once every other day and continued for two weeks. On each alternate day, at precisely 6:00AM I was awakened by the key note or musical

THIS SIDE FOR STUDENT NOTES

sound which I have through experience come to associate with my wondrously wise Venusian mentor Lon-Zara. Immediately after his precious signal brought my mind eagerly to attention, a beam or ray of light energy was focused upon my higher brain centers—the Pituitary and Pineal—by the Wise Ones, and instantly thought communication between the Venusian and myself became possible. Communications by Telethot lasted for approximately a half hour each time, after which the ray was withdrawn and our contact terminated.

During each of these thrilling sessions, when I was "in the light" and mentally attuned to Lon-Zara of Venus, my mind was illumined with a vast and wonderful wealth of HEALTH KNOWLEDGE which, if rightly used by the people of Earth, could be the positive means of banishing Dis-Ease forever on this planet. For Venusian secrets of health are simple, but dynamic. They reveal a "Law of Health" that is absolute and universal. That such a law exists, has always existed, is a true and undying fact. You, I, all humanity can use it not only to achieve a freedom from pain, but to build better, more perfect bodies.

Venusians have long known of this basic "Law of Health" and would have given it to Earthlings centuries ago if man on this planet had been sufficiently AWAKE in mind, body and soul to make wise use of it. Unhappily, we were not ready then to receive it as long as we, as a race, were following the Path of Sensation instead of the higher Path of Spiritual Wisdom.

Today, however, the pendulum is swinging the other way, from darkness to light, and a great many wonderful men and women are voluntarily searching to know CAUSES instead of EFFECTS. A great NATURAL HEALTH MOVEMENT is beginning to take hold, and noble, sincere, altruistic souls like yourselves, dear friends, are in the forefront of this mighty movement. You are demanding eternal KNOWLEDGE based on true CAUSES...not mere "information" and useless "pap" based on EFFECTS, symptoms, man-made theories, chemical drug concoctions and a greed for money.

What is the Venusian "Law of Health?" I inquired of Lon-Zara telepathically.

"In one word-BALANCE," answered my instructor. "If you require two words to better understand this Law, I would say: LIFETRONIC BALANCE. If three words are needed we can state it as: LIFETRONIC BALANCED BEING. If four words will help to further expand your understanding of it, they are: TOTAL LIFETRONIC BALANCED BEING. This law of health is established by the Cosmic Creator and is divinely ordained to apply to all animate or lining creatures, regardless of what world they may

THIS SIDE FOR STUDENT NOTES

happen to live in. Man is powerless to change it, but he can reap great benefits from the law once he KNOWS what it is all about so that he may use it for his physical betterment.

"All living creatures, including those in the sea, express themselves in four natural ways. Namely, by (1) thinking, (2) moving, (3) breathing, and (4) eating. These life activities can be called the FOUR VITAL FUNCTIONS: THOUGHT, MOTION, BREATHING and NUTRITION in all living creatures.

"Lifetrons—the vital sparks of Life' it self—enter into the physical, mental and spiritual being of roan and animals by means of the MIND, MOTION, BREATH and FOOD. Although the animals have all of the four vital functions, the first function, MIND, is lacking in conscious direction and cannot reach the heights of the development of MIND in man.

"Long ago the wise men of Venus discovered that the one Great Principle of Health for man (and animals) consists in a BALANCED, NATURAL EXPRESSION of the four vital functions. If any one of these natural life expressions is neglected by any individual, nature's LIFETRONIC BALANCE in that being is upset and the physical body will react with Dis-Ease – lack of Ease – until the natural BALANCE is once more restored. We call this the HEALTH PYRAMID PRINCIPLE, in the sense that healthy bodies have four vital functions just as a pyramid has four sides. Let me expand this idea for you."

(NOTE BY MICHAEL X: At this point, Lon-Zara energized my faculty of clairvoyance or "mental television". He then proceeded to illustrate his idea by means of six unusually Interesting and Illuminating diagrams. Since these diagrams explain how the HEALTH PYRAMID PRINCIPLE works, I have included them for you on the next page of this course. They will be mentioned by number, and you may refer to them as often as required in order to fix them clearly in mind.)

"Lifetronic balance is upset when any of the four sides of the HEALTH PYRAMID becomes OVER-DEVELOPED at the expense of the other three. The diagram I will now show you illustrate clearly what happens to the individual who has not become consciously AWARE of the importance of an even, equal, balanced development of all four sides. (The 4 vital functions.)

THIS SIDE FOR STUDENT NOTES

The Health Pyramid Principle

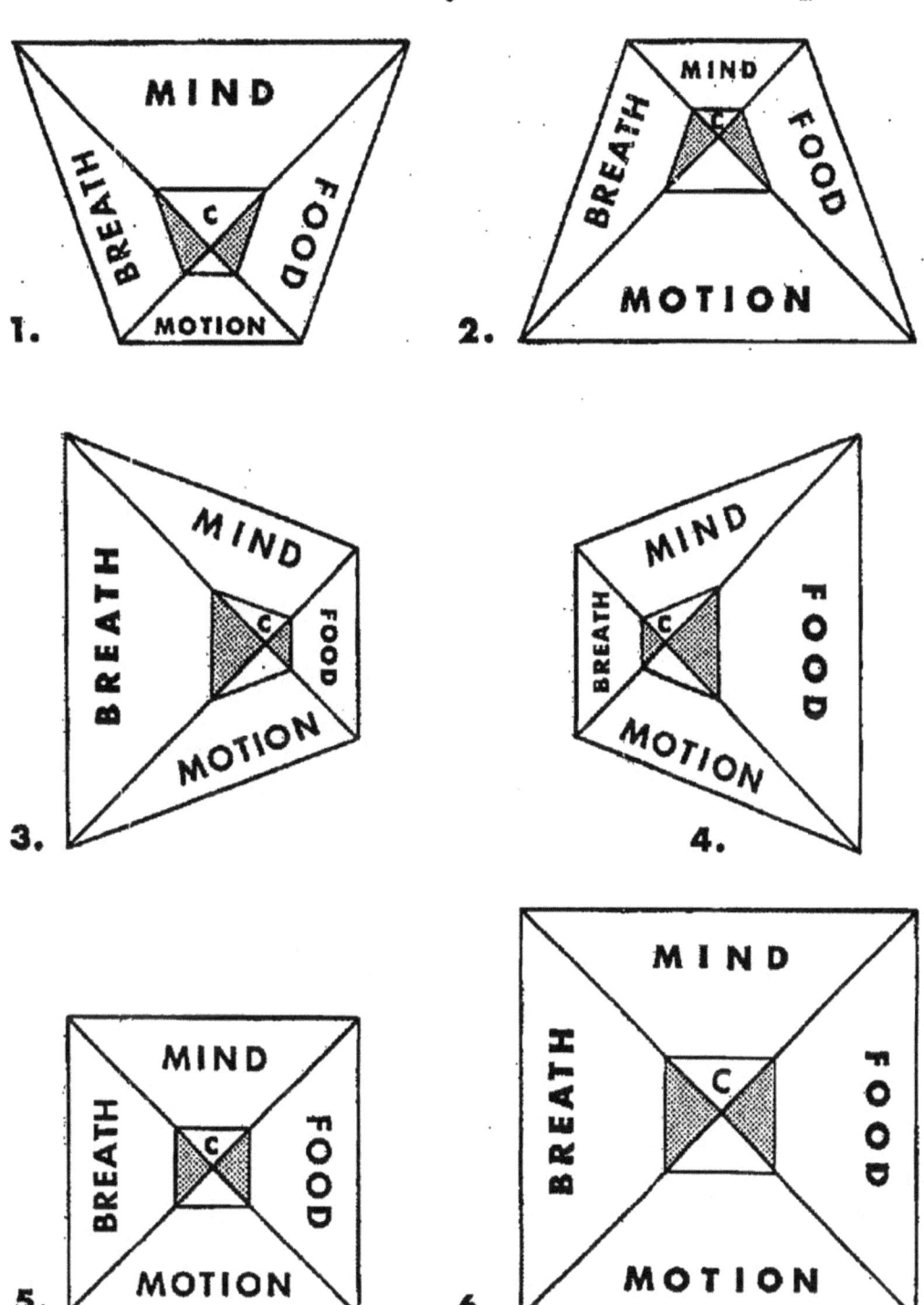

THIS SIDE FOR STUDENT NOTES

"The first diagram (1) shows a person who is over-developed in MIND function. Notice how the upper portion of the HEALTH PYRAMID is greatly expanded and enlarged, indicating that this type of individual loves to think and theorize, but does not realize the necessity for ACTION. Hence, the mentality is developed by constant study of books. However, thought alone, even though stimulated by reading the finest of books on health, is not enough to build a happy, healthy life. The "health thinker" must expand the MOTION function by more physical activity and thereby balance thinking with DOING, constructive new Ideas should be acted upon promptly.

"The second diagram (2) represents the person who relies almost exclusively upon MOTION or exercise to keep him healthy. He is the typical athlete who takes great pride in acquiring large bulging muscles. Because he feels that activity alone is the main key to good health, he neglects the development of his MIND function. This attitude swings his attention too far away from the mental side of life. He thereby shuts himself off from the healthful inflow of Spiritual Insight and ideas which he needs in order to wisely control his physical power.

"The third diagram (3) signifies the 'Breatharian'. He is the individual who is convinced that BREATH is the most important vital function for health. Yogi breathing practices intrigue him greatly. Deep breathing is more important to him than eating, and so he over-develops the BREATH function and neglects the question of right food. As a natural consequence, the ascetic breather has very little knowledge of vital food, proper combinations, etc. By neglecting the FOOD side of the health pyramid, he deprives his body of needed chemical elements which the physical body requires in order to carry the vital electric current throughout the body most efficiently. Living cells in the body need two kinds of stimulation for life and expansion: Vital and Chemical. The vital (electrical or Lifetronic) comes from the air via the BREATH function. The chemical stimulation is derived from the food we eat and the liquid we drink. The 'Breatharian' should seek to BALANCE these two functions for better health.

"The fourth diagram (4) shows a person who is very definitely over-balanced in the FOOD function. He breathes very little as he is usually too busy eating. In this classification we find the 'gourmands', 'gluttons', and also the 'Food Faddists'. These persons hold the false belief that HEALTH may be found via the FOOD path alone, or that food is the most important consideration for well-being. While it is true that good food is essential to good health, it is also true that eating is but one of the FOUR vital functions in all living creatures. To emphasize any one and ignore or minimize the

THIS SIDE FOR STUDENT NOTES

others is a serious error. It is natural and good for us to eat and enjoy delicious tasting foods, and to make sure that our food is as vital and wholesome as possible. But to fall into the habit of overeating, even of good food, is wrong because we thereby overburden the organs of digestion and lay the foundation for Dis-Ease. To correct the habit of overeating, gradually give up the old diet of cooked foods and begin eating natural, unfired fruits, nuts and tender vegetables.

"The body will demand less of these foods because they are richer in vital elements since they have not been subjected to destructive action of fire. The FOODIST will find better health by switching to the use of live, vital food and taking in more AIR through exercise. We suggested a gradual 'switch', but if he prefers a complete and sudden change to Live Food, good.

"Now we come to the fifth diagram (5) which indicates an even, progressively equal development of all four sides of the Health Pyramid. This represents the person who has not over-developed any side of the Pyramid, but has wisely built up all four sides symmetrically. He or she has exercised each of the four vital functions – MIND, MOTION, BREATH and FOOD—in a sensible, harmonious and natural manner. The happy and Joyous result is BALANCE and not DISTORTION of the Health Pyramid. A great inflow of Health-giving Lifetrons is realized by this person, from all four vital functions. As you will at once perceive, this diagram really symbolizes the New Age Student.

"The last diagram (6) is now before you. It does not, however, signify the final health attainment of man. No such finality exists in all the cosmos. One can extend the four sides of the Health Pyramid equally in the desired direction of ever greater and more abundant health. Venusian master healers have done this. A limited number of your fellow Earthlings have also achieved this goal. It is open to all mankind. As you can see in this diagram, the four vital functions of MIND, MOTION, BREATH AND FOOD have been greatly enhanced, equally. Lifetronic Balance has been maintained all during the greater development of the individuals natural functions.

"What you have revealed thus far has brought new light of understanding to my mind regarding Jim's physical breakdown," I said as Lon-Zara brought our Telethot communication to a close. "He has simply gotten out of LIFETRONIC BALANCE. But tell me, please, what is the meaning of the CAPSTONE on the Health Pyramid?" (Note: indicated by letter "C" on diagrams.)

THIS SIDE FOR STUDENT NOTES

VENUSIAN HEALTH SCIENCE & VENUSIAN SECRET SCIENCE

"I shall reveal that at our next mental meeting," replied the masterful Venusian. "Until then, you can be of great service to Jim Lindy by telling him all that you have learned during this meeting. Teach him the truth of the Wise Ones."

With those inspiring words vibrating in my mind, our mental contact was terminated, for the time being.

When I told Jim about the HEALTH PYRAMID PRINCIPLE of equal and harmonious development of the four vital functions, he grasped the idea at once. Moreover, he quickly realized in which .functions he was OVER-BALANCED (it was in MIND and FOOD functions) and he lost no time in doing everything he could to restore a more complete LIFETRONIC BALANCE.

By steadily increasing his capacity for MOTION by enjoyable outdoor exercise, my determined friend Jim thereby increased his BREATH capacity. The result was truly amazing. Not only did he begin to look better and feel better, but our backyard garden, which never before had had such wonderful care, was becoming a beautiful sight to behold.

THIS SIDE FOR STUDENT NOTES

RAISING THE TRUE CAPSTONE

Part Seven

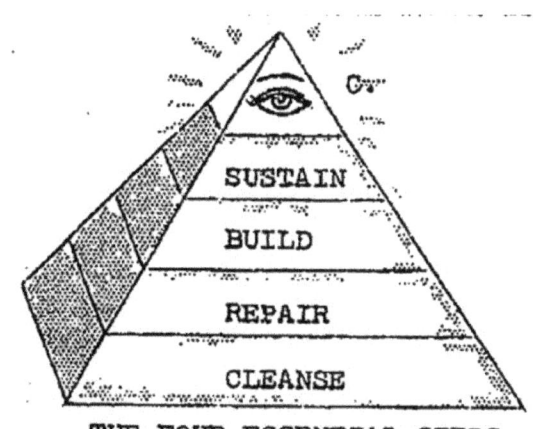

THE FOUR ESSENTIAL STEPS LEADING TO THE CAPSTONE.

WHEN Lon-Zara next contacted me telepathically, my puzzlement as to the meaning of the Capstone at the apex, of the HEALTH PYRAMID soon vanished. According to Lon-Zara, the Capstone indicates TRUTH EMBODIED, the apex to which each of the four sides of the Pyramid are rising. New Age Man will build harmoniously and simultaneously from all four sides - MIND, MOTION, BREATH and FOOD, ever, raising his awareness UPWARD to the SPIRIT OP TRUTH which is the DIVINE SELF in man. This Capstone is also known as the CHRIST CONSCIOUSNESS or "Awareness of Harmonious Perfection", it is a realization of the three principles of Power, Love and Wisdom (Life, Love and Light) as they express themselves in perfect BALANCE.

Ill health comes when man builds inharmoniously, in an unbalanced manner. The four sides of the Health pyramid are then UNEQUAL. If any side dominates or fails any other of the sides, the apex (C) cannot be reached.

The Pyramid itself, Lon-Zara pointed out to me, signifies the grander, more permanently enduring physical body each one of us is to build out of vital NEW AGE FOODS. To attempt to heal, repair, or build an AGE BODY out of OLD AGE FOODS is utterly useless, it simply cannot be done. If your "building materials are first class,

THIS SIDE FOR STUDENT NOTES

your "house" will not only look so much nicer to others...it will also last longer by many years.

By NEW AGE FOODS the Venusians mean LIVING FOODS from the plant kingdom, such as fruits, nuts, seed sprouts and tender vegetables. For physical body healing, repair and "new construction" these foods are to be eaten just as they come to us from nature, uncooked. The moment we apply fire to food we convert nature's bounty into so much dead, clogging bulk. It is clearly impossible to build LIVING BODIES OUT OF DEAD FOODS.

CHANGE OVER FROM COOKED TO NATURAL FOOD

This requires sensible planning and good Judgment. The natural, Un-Fired Food Dietary should not be taken up before cleansing the body. Casting out old matter Is the first step.

In the drawing at the beginning of this chapter, I have illustrated for you the four essential steps leading to perfect HEALTH. Just as my friend Jim Lindy was instructed to do, so each one of us roust boldly and courageously CLEANSE the physical body of its old-age matter, impurities and wastes. During this cleansing period, while the body is getting rid of old poisons that have formed in the bloodstream from the wrong foods eaten in the past, some unpleasant side-effects may be felt. These include headaches, possibly nausea and a temporary recurrence of old symptoms. When the body has rid itself of its wastes, such symptoms disappear. This takes time, however, and if this natural eliminative REACTION is not understood, one might lose faith and sink back to old ways.

For this reason I consider it most unwise for the average beginner to give up all the old foods at once. Unless the beginner is a person strong in will and self-discipline and willing to undergo a few periods of unpleasant eliminative reactions, he or she should GRADUALLY change over to the vital, LIVE FOOD program. Do it by degrees, little by little. Then there will be fewer noticeable physical disturbances. In making your transition from cooked to NATURAL foods it is best to begin with such foods as are not commonly cooked. This would include a great variety of delicious fresh fruits - apples, oranges, persimmons, apricots, cherries, melons, and many others. Fruits are best at the peak of their season (which you will soon get to recognize as you watch for them on the market) and your own taste buds are the most perfect guides for you to follow whenever you are hungry. (After the body has undergone its cleansing.)

THIS SIDE FOR STUDENT NOTES

Begin to add vital, UN-FIRED foods little by little to your present dietary. As you do this, the natural foods, the delicious tasting fruits, nuts, sprouted seeds and mixed green salads with tender vegetables, all uncooked, will become more and more attractive and desirable to your taste. That is a splendid sign. You will soon find that you are automatically substituting more unfired, natural foods for the cooked ones. At times, let a complete meal consist of one or two fresh fruits. Let another meal be a salad of green leafy lettuce, cucumbers, tomatoes and avocado, with an olive-oil and lemon dressing.

Incidentally, you may think you enjoy cooked food, but as many New Age individuals, including Jim and myself have discovered, a person doesn't know REAL food enjoyment until he or she gets to enjoying sun-energized food Just as Nature prepares It, entirely without a "cook stove". Not only is it most satisfying and pleasing to the palate, but it also adds those vital elements to our bodies that the well meaning cook with her or his, destructive FIRE has been depriving us of for YEARS.

After several months, possibly sooner, of this procedure, substituting tasty natural foods for cooked foods you will reach the stage of not wanting any more cooked foods of any kind - They will no longer taste alive and vital to you. Then you will naturally desire to eat only natural, un-fired foods exclusively, for you will be sure you are on the right track at last. When this day arrives, you will indeed rejoice.

In the matter of FOOD, balance is vitally important. Do not try to live on fruits alone, nor on vegetables alone. You need both to build your NEW AGE BODY. Fruits alone provide too little of tissue-building material. Vegetables are the best builders because they get the roost minerals from the soil. The FRUITS CLEANS and VEGETABLES BUILD. A splendid plan, then, would be to eat fruits in the morning, sprouts and leafy greens at noon and a small salad of root vegetables in the evening.

Live for one year on these foods and you will find your vitality greatly increased. After two years you will be amazed at the extraordinary keenness of your mental faculties. In three years time you will be surprised to note that most of your wrinkles have "gone forever" and that you possess unusual strength. And after five years you will realize that you have stopped "Father Time" in his tracks. You are REGENERATED.

Remember, build your "house" upon a "rock" of principle and it will stand firm. In this case, principle is LIFE...as found in LIVING FOODS. Live food from the plant kingdom gives you FIRST CLASS material with which to build your house (physical

THIS SIDE FOR STUDENT NOTES

body). So I can only echo the practical advice of our marvelous SPACE BROTHERS AND SISTERS by saying, Build your new house out of the BEST, not inferior grade material! This brings us to the question of MEAT-EATING. On this, Lon-Zara was quite definite.

"Our life comes from the Sun, via its Lifetronic activity in the atmosphere of each planet. Solar energy is the source, mediate and immediate, of all plant and animal life. The sun severs the carbon from its oxygen and builds the vegetable.

The animal consumes the vegetable, a RE-UNION of the severed elements takes place, producing animal vitality. The process of building a vegetable is one of WINDING UP Lifetronic energy from the sun's rays. The process of building an animal is one of RUNNING DOWN or the using of that wound-up solar energy. As you know, the green leaves of plants trap solar rays and store up the electrical energy for the purpose of building and vitalizing the plant.

"Centuries ago, the greatest minds of Venus had taught our people that man's natural food is that which comes from the plant and from the animal kingdom. We knew that it was better to obtain our vital life energy from FIRST-HAND SOURCES such as plants, than to eat animals that secured their vitality by eating plants. Remember, the process of building up an animal is one of RUNNING DOWN of Solar Energy. When the flesh of any animal is cooked, Lifetrons are dispelled into the air and very little of the original life electricity is left for the healthful, vital invigoration of a human being.

"We observe you Earthlings eating meat and cooked food and getting sick with many diseases, the cause of which baffles you and your scientists. We can tell you authoritatively that the reason for your mysterious diseases is your racial custom of eating the dead corpses of animals. The moment an animal is killed, the electric vitality that sustained its tissues when it was alive, rapidly dissipates into the atmosphere. In order to decompose the dead flesh, and reduce it to its chemical elements, putrefactive germs enter the meat and a process you call rotting occurs. At a certain point in the disintegration process, an almost invisible agent of destruction, the Scavenger Virus takes over and completes the decomposition.

"Nature never keeps anything she isn't using. This is the universal law of use. Hence, dead animals are speedily decomposed by the germs and scavenger virus, so that the original chemical elements that built the animal's body will be available again for more constructive work. If you will always think of the scavenger virus (and all

THIS SIDE FOR STUDENT NOTES

germs) as Nature's 'clean-up agents', the necessity for their being becomes evident. When earthlings break the natural law of diet by eating the dead flesh of animals, birds and fishes instead of obtaining their food from the plant kingdom, what happens? First, the flesh goes into the human stomach. The gastric Juices paralyze the action of numerous germs which the meat contains. The meat then passes into the intestines which, contrary to common belief, do not absorb the flesh at all but merely absorb its juices. In the warm interior of the human body, the putrefactive germs begin to multiply by the billions to decompose the meat, if man's intestinal tract were short, as is that of a dog, this putrefactive or rotting activity would not be so harmful. Man's intestines, however, are several times longer than a canine's. They were designed and intended by the infinite Creator for the purpose of digesting fruits, nuts, seeds and vegetables which DO NOT COME UNDER THE LAW OF THE SCAVENGER VIRUS. Because the putrefying meat cannot be excreted rapidly enough from the human intestines, the scavenger virus has no alternative than to finish the decomposing of the meat inside the body of man. This it does, thereby releasing into the human bloodstream poisons of a most virulent and destructive kind. It is no wonder that the cells of a human body become diseased under that poisonous onslaught which goes on day after day."

These health reasons, not commonly known by Earthlings, should be compelling enough to make many souls of good intent turn away forever the dangerous habit of flesh-eating. But the Venusians go further and appeal to Man's higher nature (Life, Love and Wisdom) to not betray our younger-brothers (animals) by killing and eating them, but to protect them with CHRIST LOVE!

THIS SIDE FOR STUDENT NOTES

MODULATING YOURSELF UPWARD

Part Eight

JIM Lindy was making splendid progress. In the few short months that had passed so adventurously for my guest, definite sign of improvement were noticeable. His mind, body and soul were manifesting a greater harmony, balance and a joyous "positivity". It was outwardly apparent to me now that Jim had succeeded in his important objective: namely, to "cross the Three Rivers".

Not that the job was accomplished. We realized that much remained to be done in order for Jim to keep the health gains he had made so far. Also, it was vitally important to continue further expansion into health by learning whatever else our Higher Brothers - the Venusians - would reveal to us. At every opportunity I made it a point to compliment Jim on his wonderful improvement in health...and I meant every word.

He no longer looked like a "walking dead man". Life now radiated from his sparkling eyes as never before. Of course, true to Jim Lindy's nature (as I had always known him) he took little or no personal credit for the marvelous physical transformation. The Space People, Dr. C, Lenore and I, were responsible, he claimed. Yet I knew that if it were not for Jim's own unconquerable desire to be well again and his loyalty to the Space People's instruction he might never have made it. That is Jim's way.

Somehow, subconsciously, Jim knew that God and Nature never intended for him or any human being to be in the pitiful condition he was when he first came to see me. The bad experiences he had gone through in searching for a cure had hurt and confused him. Yet even when he was at his "wits end" he still believed help would come. And so it did. The Higher Brothers take care of their own. That is their way.

THIS SIDE FOR STUDENT NOTES

My next communication from Lon-Zara opened up the most delightful new "health vistas" for both Jim and myself. So unusual and valuable was the knowledge he imparted to me, I shall present it here for you as clearly as I can. It gives us all the key to LIFE MORE ABUNDANT. And that means knowing the SECRET that can change your whole body chemistry, release you from the unhappy burden of "dragging through life" half alive. Practicing the secret gives you a PATTERN OF UPLIFT so powerful and positive it cannot fail to help you manifest much greater health, strength and youthfulness. It is this:

THE LAW OF BEING IS VIBRATION. As the Wise Ones say - "Everything vibrates". The world is not static and inactive. It is alive, dynamic and very, very ACTIVE. The Venusians have learned that it is easier to live in ACTIVITY than to exist in laziness. From the tiniest particle of matter, the electron, up to the greatest galactic universe in space...all is in MOTION. And everything in the universe has its own identifying vibration. Especially living human beings.

Does any law control vibration? Yes. According to Lon-Zara the law of vibration is MODULATION. A simple example of modulation is had when you vary the tone of your voice. You have then "modulated" the intensity or power of your voice, and perhaps even changed its frequency or rate of vibration from high to low, low to medium, etc. It is all very simple. You do it every day, and with the greatest of ease.

Now the important thing the Venusians want us to know is HOW TO MODULATE or "change" our individual personal vibrations, physical, mental and spiritual, from low, to medium, to high. The secret of doing this is to realize that every other vibration outside of us tends to modulate us either UPWARD or DOWNWARD. This "modulation" of our personal vibrations goes on continually, affecting us negatively or positively depending on whether the influencing vibration is high, medium or low.

The range of vibrations in the universe is considerable. Hence we needn't try to list them all here, except to say that vibrations come in "Octaves" (variations of eight) in the universal scheme of things. Lon-Zara refers to them as "hidden Octaves of Power". Some vibrations, however, have much higher frequency (rate of vibration) than others. For HEALTH MAGIC, the most important Octaves for you to remember are:

58th Octave: Thought Waves

50th Octave: Lifetrons, Live Food Enzymes

THIS SIDE FOR STUDENT NOTES

48th Octave: Live cells of human body

Why are these so important? Because if you eat a meal that vibrates below the 40th Octave, it is "deader" than you are. Therefore, it modulates you DOWNWARD, (Cooked food is far below the 40th Octave). This affects your health adversely because lower vibrations SLOW DOWN THE MOTION of your whole being, body, mind and soul. For example, Jim Lindy had previously believed that a dietary of well-cooked foods with plenty of meat was benefiting his health. It; was not until serious physical ills began to trouble him that he opened his mind to the simple truth, which was ONLY LIVING FOODS ADD LIFE TO A LIVING BODY. Dead foods prevent the life force from healing the body.

Jim Lindy "crossed the First River" by gradually learning how to clear his mind of a huge amount of mental rubbish that was hindering him from thinking dearly. By coming into personal contact with positive NEW VIBRATIONS – those of the Venusians, Dr. C, Lenore (my wonderful housekeeper) and myself – Jim's mind was modulated UPWARD, instead of constantly thinking of negative EFFECTS, he reversed his attention to a positive new realm, that of CAUSES.

Vibrations should always LIFT us. They should not be allowed to pull us downward. or to reduce our VITAL POWER- You can modulate your life into whatever you want it to be, just as Jim did. For you are the Selector of the Octave that you wish to affect you. I have no control of that, nor do the Space People have any influence in that respect" It is up to you alone to decide whether you wish to live in a valley or upon a glorious MOUNTAIN TOP!

Modulation is the secret key to your success and health. How do you use it in everyday, practical living? Like this:

Be aware of the fact that colors affect you, sounds affect you, music affects you, your friends, relatives and companions affect you. That is not all. Books, magazines, newspapers affect you; groups and meetings, movies, "TV" shows, the food you eat, your household surroundings, your church...all of these vibrations modulate you- either UPWARD or DOWNWARD.

Take away that which modulates YOU downward, and add that which modulates you UPWARD. It is as simple as that. But in its very simplicity lies its POWER.

THIS SIDE FOR STUDENT NOTES

"Build a Pattern of Uplift", said Lon-Zara. "If you would truly move Onward, Upward and Godward. You react to everything that touches you. Nothing you contact leaves you unchanged. Its vibrations modulate you either up or down. So you must personally direct this modulation process In the positive direction of greater physical health, strength and vitality. Every thought you think, every meal you eat, every companion and experience should be UPLIFTING."

When Jim Lindy became aware of this unique health secret, he put it into actual practice at once by seeking and. enjoying all wholesome influences which had the power to uplift. Destructively negative television plays and movies dealing with crime, horror and sudden death, Jim listed as "taboo". And, In the matter of diet he willingly gave up the old habit of eating meat which, he realized, only modulated him downward. In taking this step, giving up meat, he "crossed the second river" by lifting and purifying his desires with a true CHRIST LOVE.

To his surprise it was not as difficult to give up meat as he had imagined. Once the low vibration of the animal flesh that had been saturating his bloodstream for years, was replaced by the higher vibration from fresh fruits, nuts, vegetables and sprouted seeds, his craving for animal meat disappeared. After a few months away from meat entirely, his bloodstream vibration was so pure and high that the very sight or thought of eating dead animal flesh disgusted him.

Jim was fast becoming a "New Age Earthling". He realized that Vegetarianism, while of great importance, is only the first upward step in the complete New Age Dietary Program. It is also highly important to gradually discontinue the use of ALL COOKED FOODS. Every cooked food has been deprived of most of its LIFE ingredients – Lifetrons, enzymes, vitamins, and organic minerals. Hence, cooked foods modulate us DOWNWARD.

Unfortunately, most sincere Vegetarians do not know of this law of MODULATION and so they eat numerous cooked foods such as breads, cookies, potatoes (baked, boiled, mashed, etc) "meat substitutes" "gravy substitutes", soy beans, and as a result are often very poor examples of health. The Venusians tell us that what we should all do is to see that EVERYTHING we add to our diet RAISES THE LIFE VIBRATION!"

"Very good," you say, "but I can't always get the kind of 100# LIVE, VITAL MEALS you and Lon-Zara recommend. I have to eat what is served to me, and it is mostly cooked food. Is there any way of increasing the LIFE vibration in my diet?"

THIS SIDE FOR STUDENT NOTES

Happily, there is. It is not as good as being able to eat your true natural food in the raw, unfired state, but it will see you through until you can improve your situation. Here is ray suggestion. If you DO eat something of a lower vibration at any time, see that you BALANCE it with a larger amount of a higher vibration food. A splendid way of doing this is to gradually increase your intake of fresh, raw, vegetable juices. Carrot juice (a large glassful) can be taken a half-hour before each meal. This will give you extra enzymes and Lifetrons to step up the vibrations of the other foods.

Let's look in briefly once again on Jim Lindy's progress.

By following the cell cleansing program each month as Lon-Zara had suggested, (1st day on pure water only; 2nd day on diluted fresh fruit juices; 3rd day a choice of any desired fresh, uncooked juicy fruit in season). Jim had gradually cleansed find purified his body and thereby "crossed the Third River" to his own great joy. He knew now that there would be no "turning back."

If you, like Jim Lindy, sincerely seek to RAISE your vibrations by taking away that which pulls you downward and adding that which LIFTS YOU UPWARD…if you MODULATE YOURSELF UPWARD by continually making right choices, in this respect, your HEALTH progress will soon amaze you, and all who know you!

IMPORTANT ANSWERS REGARDING YOUR "NEW AGE DIET"

Q. If I discontinue the eating of animal meat, fish, and poultry, where shall I get my required protein?

A. FIRST RATE sources of natural CLEAN protein include Alfalfa sprouts (contain up to 50% MORE protein than wheat) Fenugreek sprouts, Mung bean sprouts, Sunflower seeds, and nuts such as Almond, Filbert, Pecan, Walnut. Nuts should be eaten fresh and raw, never roasted or salted. We eat them flaked.

Q, Are Dairy Products-milk, cream, and cheese used?

A. All animal foods and by-products of same, including eggs are gradually discontinued from the New Age Diet. We replace those items (which are not man's true foods) with ALMOND NUT MILK and CREAM. This is so delicious and satisfying; you will find no difficulty in substituting the NEW for the OLD. Here is the recipe for ALMOND NUT MILK or CREAM:

THIS SIDE FOR STUDENT NOTES

1 pint distilled water

1 heaping tbsp. fresh, raw Almond butter

1 scant tbsp. natural unheated honey

1 teaspoon whole Anise seed

Directions: Put the above ingredients in your blender or liquefier and let whirl at high speed for 25 minutes—this makes a delicious, rich milk. To make a rich cream, simply use less water, or add a little more Almond butter. It is quite palatable without straining but if used for infants it should be strained. This will keep about four days if refrigerated. Use in small amounts as beverage, add to carrot juice for a smooth flavor. This milk or cream is highly nutritious and tasty on sliced apples, peaches, persimmons, berries, and other fresh fruit in season, or on dried fruits. Good in fig juice.

Q. Is bread necessary in this New Age Diet?

A. No! According to Lon-Zara, bread is an unwholesome food since it has been subjected to the high temperature of the baking oven. Venusian people eat no bread of any kind. The occasional use of hard, dry whole-grain crackers is a good way to gradually break away from the bread-eating habit. A natural food far superior to bread is tender young corn. It can be immersed two minutes in hot water, or eaten raw. Never cook it.

Q. Why is it that, although food is abundant in this country, surveys indicate that from one-half to two-thirds of our population is underfed?

A. One can eat food all day long, but if that food has been cooked or processed it is lacking in real nourishment.

Q. Are fats needed in the New Age Diet?

A. If you mean natural fats, yes. Natural fats are those which are uncooked, such as are in avocadoes, seeds and nuts of all kinds. The fat in these foods is unsaturated and easily emulsified by the liver. Unsaturated fats are also found in all cold-pressed natural oils, such as safflower seed oil, sesame seed oil, soy bean oil, olive oil, peanut oil, corn oil, etc. All these natural fats are wholesome and beneficial in the diet. (We recommend using them on salads with lemon and honey, but not as emulsified or mayonnaise type dressings.) On the other hand, ALL COOKED FATS are always

THIS SIDE FOR STUDENT NOTES

unwholesome and have a dangerous tendency to clog the human arteries with cholesterol. The cooked or saturated fats include butter, meat fat, egg yolks, cheese and commercial shortenings. Most Americans eat one to two cups of this saturated grease every day in their foods.

They fill up on ham or bacon and eggs for breakfast, buttered toast; they eat heavily of cheese, gravy, whipped cream, and meats (even lean meat has 20% fat) and of course ice cream. Quite naturally, all this adds up. In a year's time the average person consumes 300 or more cups of cholesterol-forming saturated FAT. Think of the result in five, ten or fifteen years of such a diet! Cooked fats cannot be used by the human body, and in our opinion, do untold harm to the liver and gallbladder as well as the arteries. None of the Venusians eat cooked fats and consequently never suffer from strokes, liver disease, or heart attacks.

Q. Do you use salt or other condiments on your salads?

A. Raw foods have their own delicate natural flavor and so the use of salt or pepper is never required. By cooking his food, man makes it flat and insipid to the taste, and in order to remedy this mistake he resorts to the use of salt and other irritating condiments. Ordinary table salt (sodium chloride) is an inorganic substance and so cannot be assimilated by the human body. It can only irritate. It is like sand in the gears of a precision machine; it grinds in the gears (bony joints) and slowly but surely damages the machine. The body needs sodium, but in ORGANIC form only. Richest sources of organic sodium are raw spinach, celery and beet greens. Include these Items in your diet, plus plenty of raw vegetable juices, and all craving for salt - will disappear. For salads mix equal amounts olive oil and lemon juice, add a small clove of garlic and sweeten with small amount of natural honey.

THIS SIDE FOR STUDENT NOTES

MAGIC OF THE GOLDEN SPHERE

Part Nine

EVER since his first Bream Contact from the Venusians, Jim Lindy's purpose was three-fold. He intensely desired to follow their instructions as perfectly as possible, to regain his physical health and then raise his vibrations into a higher frequency. By making the few positive changes that had already been suggested, Jim had made real "headway" in body, mind and soul. As a result, he was permitted to once again sense the presence of the Wise Ones in a second Dream Contact.

THE SECOND DREAM CONTACT

An exquisitely beautiful GOLDEN SPHERE in this Dream Contact was the vision which Jim related to me as follows; "First of all I became aware of a most unusual vibration around me. It was like warm, healing sunshine... so harmonious and peaceful I wanted to bask in it forever. Then I saw a tiny point of light. It gradually increased in size until it had assumed the form of a GOLDEN SPHERE, 12 inches in diameter. It glowed and radiated with a golden luminescence as it floated through space in my direction.

"I heard a clear, bell-like voice speak as the GOLDEN SPHERE moved toward me. That spoken word was SUSTAIN! Automatically I reached out my hands and caught the GOLDEN SPHERE. As soon as I did so, my entire body began to radiate a golden glow. In that glorious moment I felt Godlike, conscious of the most wonderful Life and Intelligence and Perfect Protection. Then the vision faded and I awoke."

This whole, inner experience, though occurring in a deep sleep state Just as before, was not at all like ordinary dream adventures. There was a positive sense of

THIS SIDE FOR STUDENT NOTES

REALITY and VIVIDNESS about it that dreams usually lack. Most important, no mere dream carries the HIGH VIBRATIONS that Jim Lindy felt in every atom and fiber of his being long after he awakened. At my next opportunity I eagerly inquired of Lon-Zara regarding the practical significance of Jim's second vision. What I learned was as astonishing as it was thrilling.

"When an Earthling whom we have embraced within our auric circle of protection, becomes ill in body, mind or spirit, the first thing we do for that individual is to RAISE HIS OR HER LIFE SWITCH. That opens the channel through which a great abundance of Lifetrons can pour into the human body. As you know, our devoted Earth Brother, Dr. C, is one of the principal channels through which this vitally important healing service is performed. By residing on Earth as 'one of you' he is enabled to carry on this essential work of bringing diseased and broken bodies back into Lifetronic Balance. Only then can those sincere individuals be of real service to the Cosmic Plan and their fellowmen. Lifetronic Balance is basic.

"We next instruct the health seeker as to the proper method of crossing the 'Three Rivers'. By this we mean, of course, the CLEANSING of one's thoughts, the transmuting of one's desires from low vibrations to high vibrations, and the purifying of the living cells of the physical body.

"Not long after the sincere Earthling has accomplished these necessary procedures, and is beginning to experience a marked improvement in his health, we project to him a GOLDEN SPHERE. This sphere is most often sent to the individual during his normal sleep state at night. It is perceived at once by the subliminal awareness of the one to whom we direct it. This perception is not imaginary but very real."

"What are the virtues of the GOLDEN SPHERE?" I asked.

"Its primary purpose is to MODULATE the vibrations of the one who receives it. The modulation is powerfully UPWARD. That is because our GOLDEN SPHSRE carries a HIGH CHARGE of the healing Lifetrons. Its directive is to vitalize, protect and enlighten. (Power, Love and Wisdom). Therefore the effect of the GOLDEN SPHERE is always highly positive and invigorating.

"The sphere has another significance. Its golden color indicates spiritual influence. When the Subliminal mind or Soul contacts THE GOLDEN SPHERE, during the Dream-Contact, its awareness of the great importance of the trinity powers—Life, Love and Intelligence—is vastly increased. For it is by virtue of

THIS SIDE FOR STUDENT NOTES

BALANCED USE of those three principles that each one of us becomes a radiantly healthy, joyous being, able to expand our personal SPHERE OF SPIRITUAL INFLUENCE. Within the sphere, the trinity powers of Life, Love and Light are in colors of light blue, rose pink and light yellow, respectively."

Suddenly I recalled that Jim had been impressed during his Dream-Contact, by a directive to "SUSTAIN!"

"Truly," said Lon-Zara, "the physical, mental and soul progress that Jim has achieved must now be SUSTAINED. The slightest deflection downward from the HEALTH PRINCIPLES that have caused him to regain his vigor and strength, must not be permitted. There is NO TURNING BACK from the HIGH PATH once a certain degree of progress has been attained. There is only ETERNAL PROGRESSION, onward, upward and Godward. The consequences of 'turning back' from the HIGH PATH (right thoughts, actions, breath, and food) are most SEVERE. Not only would Jim's old diseases return, but his life problems would multiply."

I could see how this would be true. Lot's wife, in the Bible story, had made considerable progress on the HIGH PATH. Then one day she "looked back" (returned to wrong habits of living) and for her foolish error was turned into a pillar of salt- (Became crystallized in wrong thoughts, desires, and actions.) The result was complexity, confusion and calamity.

Jim's reaction from the GOLDEN SPHERE experience was a gradual increase in physical stamina and "pep". He slept much better and did not tire so easily. The "Paradisical Diet" of uncooked natural foods-fruits, nuts, sprouted seeds and green, leafy vegetables that Lenore prepared for Jim's breakfast, lunch and supper, were performing their LIVING MAGIC. By this simple program of natural eating, which Included plenty of delicious tasting fresh or dried (soaked overnight) fruits, green, leafy salads with young carrots, celery, beets, apples, sprouted seeds, etc., Jim Lindy began to enjoy natural elimination which he had not known for years. With more natural elimination of all food wastes, his body continued to rebuild and grow stronger.

Of course, both Jim and I were careful to build the Health Pyramid (Mind, Motion, Food and Breath) as symmetrically as possible. We knew that natural food, while mightily important, only stimulates the INTERNAL MUSCLES of the digestive and eliminative system. By exercising our EXTERNAL MUSCLES also, through brisk

THIS SIDE FOR STUDENT NOTES

walking and hill climbing in fresh air and sun, we both derived HEALTH BENEFITS beyond price.

"After you have built a new body," concluded my Venusian instructor, "you must SUSTAIN it by wise choice of foods and wholesome, healthful activities. Cease causing your body temple to suffer from unnatural, unwise habits of eating, or thinking, or feeling. Strive to modulate your life UPWARDS from now on, and never go back to the old ways that brought on your troubles originally. We know you and Jim will slip back occasionally. Even though you believed at once that man's food should not be perverted by fire and chemical processing, it may take many months of continued experimenting and testing before you are thoroughly convinced of this truth. But keep in balance as you proceed. Strive to control your food and don't allow the food to control you. You are seeking higher thrills, greater satisfaction than merely the delights of eating palatable food. I have observed your delight and keen appreciation as you bit into a juicy apple at the peak of its season. Your appreciation was for the work of Nature and the Sun. This very delight and gratefulness to Nature adds to the benefit which the natural food gives you. Let your food, like all else you contact, modulate you ever ONWARD and UPWARD in VIBRATION!"

THIS SIDE FOR STUDENT NOTES

VENUSIAN VRIL AND VITALITY

Part Ten

THERE is an ancient and honorable saying to the effect that, "The best wine is always served last". While we do not personally imbibe fermented drinks (preferring the wholesome and delicious taste of fresh grape juice), for Jim Lindy and me the "best wine" did come last. It came in the form of RARE HEALTH SECRETS from the wonderful planet VENUS.

I had just relayed to Jim the significance of his second Dream Contact in which he had experienced the power and magic of the GOLDEN SPHERE. He was very pleased to hear that Lon-Zara and the Lifetronic healers of Venus were responsible for having projected the SPHERE to him. His awareness of the presence of the Venusians had now become much keener. Although the Wise Ones had not revealed themselves to Jim in the visible, objective form as yet, he knew full well that they DO EXIST. The conviction that soon—when his personal vibrations were higher-he too would be given the glorious privilege of being a "Contactee". That is, he would be allowed to communicate consciously with the Space People, first by Telethot, then later on by actual "Contacts" physically. When that Joyous time came, he would see them as they actually appear—radiant, vibrant Godlike beings of Life, Love and Light. With a happy smile, Jim joined me for a hike.

THIS SIDE FOR STUDENT NOTES

Besides my regular before-breakfast hike on which Jim had frequently Joined me, it was our custom (suggested by Dr. C) to go for a mile hike in the afternoon twice a week. The most ideal place for this was my favorite hiking grounds-the Hollywood Hills. Usually we made no attempt to climb Mt. Hollywood (1500 ft. elev.) but satisfied ourselves with pleasant strolls near Griffith Park Observatory. But today was most unusual.

"Let's climb Mt Hollywood, Michael!" he said. "Reach the summit together. I feel up to it today and somehow I feel that this climb may prove very important to us."

We began the climb easily, resting whenever Jim or I felt the need of a "breather", and then continuing upward at a moderate pace. It was very difficult to believe that my climbing partner was the same man who a few short months back had been "at the end of his rope" physically. The very fact that he now was moving easily with me up the mountain path was living proof of the dynamic effectiveness of VENUSIAN METHODS. No longer was Jim Lindy content to remain on the lower paths of Life, for with new powers stirring within him he felt impelled to venture onward, upward to the HIGH PLACES, to the mountain tops of Life, Love and Light. Jim's impulse to climb Mt. Hollywood and reach the summit was the "outward action" that signified clearly his determination to prove himself truly worthy of the New Age knowledge he had already received.

We reached the; half-way point in about an hour. Our breathing gradually became more labored with each upward step. Whenever we noticed this, we rested a few moments to sort of catch our breath. Once, as Jim paused a long while to enjoy the beauty of the wooded landscape below, I sensed a weakening of his will to go higher. The climb was beginning to tell.

"You've never seen the magnificent view from the top of this mountain," I said. "Words don't do it justice, but if we keep climbing steadily you will soon reach the summit. The view up there puts this one to shame!"

These few words of encouragement worked wonders. Jim pushed forward again with new strength, and In spite of the struggle, soon got his "second wind". We moved higher and higher on the mountain trail, making steady progress. Less than one hour later we made the final winding turn on the trail and as we did so, both of us smiled broadly. The summit was there before us, only a hundred yards ahead! From our position on the trail we could see that another climber besides ourselves, had arrived

THIS SIDE FOR STUDENT NOTES

at the summit ahead of us. No doubt tills stranger had started earlier than we had, although we had not noticed him anywhere on the trail.

He was a tall, quiet-mannered individual. As we stepped to the crest of the mountain to feast our eyes upon the vast panorama below us—the great metropolitan city of Los Angeles, surrounded by numerous outlying towns, Glendale, Pasadena, Altadena, Whittier, etc.—he greeted us with a friendly nod of his head and the cheery remark: "Beautiful sight isn't It?"

"Indeed it is," exclaimed Jim. "Well worth the struggle it takes to get up here. If my vitality were only greater, I might consider making mountain climbing a regular hobby. But tell me, do you climb this mountain frequently?"

"Yes." The good-natured stranger continued: "And I have met some wonderful people on this very summit. To me, Mt. Hollywood is just a pleasant foothill rather than a mountain; for I have met the challenge of greater peaks in years past.

"Nearly all of them seemed almost impossible to conquer at first, but after my first few triumphs in reaching the top of each mountain successfully, I began to realize that most of us live far below our true capacity. We imagine we are unable to climb a certain mountain and so-imagination overshadows the will and we find ourselves powerless. By the simple process of 'reversing the imagination' one can learn how to turn failure into success, defeat into victory, and weakness into limitless new strength."

The stranger paused, smiled, and his large eyes sparkled like bright diamonds in the sunlight. His features were clean, even and harmonious. Physical vitality was indicated by his deep, full chest, broad shoulders and narrow, trim waist. He wore ordinary hiking clothes very similar to our own, and except for the fact that his eyes sparkled with unusual brilliance; he looked much like any other Earthling. But he talked with a deep sense of inner poise, balance and power that is rarely found In men and women of our planet.

As Jim engaged the stranger in conversation, I thought to myself, could this be a planned Contact? Hardly had the thought entered my mind when the stranger stopped his chatting with Jim, looked me directly in the eyes and said:

"Yes, Michael," speaking my name as if he had known me for some time. "I am a special agent of Lon-Zara your Venusian Instructor. My own name at the moment is unimportant. I see that both you and your companion are astonished. Do not be. For

THIS SIDE FOR STUDENT NOTES

those traveling the HIGH PATH the 'unexpected' soon becomes the rule, with each new event more unusual and thrilling than the previous one. EXPECT THE UNEXPECTED. Accredited agents from Venus are closer to Earthlings than you realize!

The stranger then told me certain details about Lon-Zara and the planet Venus which convinced me beyond a doubt that he was indeed a messenger of the Wise One I revered so dearly. He explained that the purpose of meeting us here on the summit of Mt. Hollywood, in the full light of day, was to demonstrate a VENUSIAN HEALTH PRACTICE of great importance to Jim. I too, would benefit from it, and in turn could teach it to others. In this way, the valuable practice would soon benefit many who are in great need of it and who will benefit the world by using it.

Jim Lindy was utterly speechless. The emotional impact of at last coming into personal contact with such, a being as this, well nigh "floored" him. He had hoped and prayed that the Venusians would make their physical presence known to him in some way. Still, a meeting like this, in broad daylight, was far beyond his wildest expectations.

The Venusian agent extended both hands chest high. His hands remained open, the left hand with palm facing upward and the right hand with palm facing downward.

"If you wish, you may think of this special practice as A & B Technique," he said.

"With my hands in this position, I am consciously ATTRACTING a large supply of Lifetrons directly from the atmosphere. They are entering my body through my opened left hand, and no mental effort on my part is needed to cause them to do so. If you will extend your left hand outward with palm upward, you will soon feel a tingle from the Lifetronic movement."

We did so at once and felt the tingle immediately. It signified that trillions of tiny Lifetrons were pouring into our bodies through the opened left hand. We were told that the universe is filled with vital, LIFETRONIC ENERGY ("LE") to such an abundant degree that there is more of this power available at all times than you or I could ever possibly use. We live in an ocean of LIFE ELECTRICITY. Each one of us is like a sponge in this ocean, continually absorbing all we need of "LE" for the energizing and repair of our physical bodies. Why then, do we sicken; become feeble, old and DIE SO SOON?

The amazing stranger read my thought.

THIS SIDE FOR STUDENT NOTES

"Because the majority of mankind on earth have BLOCKED this wonderful Lifetronic Energy, prevented its greater INFLOW, by not becoming AWARE OF IT mentally, physically and spiritually. Although it is true that Lifetrons enter your body even without your being aware of their activity, it is also true that you may ı step-upı your Intake of them consciously by MENTAL DIRECTION. For our HEALTH practice, ('A & B Technique') we first become aware of Lifetrons as they enter the left hand. Instantly they complete a circuit all through the body and out again through the right hand. Now let us go a step further. Let's increase POWER.

"Think of your left hand as a MAGNET FOR LIFE ENERGY. It has the power to ATTRACT Lifetrons in abundance, according to your will. 'A' in our practice, signifies ATTRACT. Think of your physical body as an OPEN CIRCUIT fed by the universe. Now Lifetronic energy flows into you, is stepped up into a higher vibration, and then sent back to the universe as your BLESSING to other life forms. Think of your right hand, then as a positive instrument by which you BLESS the universe. That is, you send out streams of Lifetrons to enliven all that grows. It is by virtue of Lifetrons that the seed germinates in the ground and grows up to become a tree with leaves, fruits and flowers. Pour streams of Lifetrons on a seed, and you quicken in a minute what would otherwise, with less of the life-force, occupy weeks to grow. A knowledge of this great living force (LE) and how to apply it, is the secret of the Venusians' radiant health and ever-joyous youthfulness. Our power is in AWARENESS. This AWARENESS is now increasing magnificently in many souls of Earth.

"'A & B Technique' has great HEALTH value for you, and for all New Age Earthlings. Its applications are infinite. You can use this method to consciously Increase your Intake of Lifetrons from the atmosphere, and pour them through your right hand into your daily food, for greater NUTRITIONAL BENEFITS. (Particularly necessary if one eats cooked food.) The liquids you drink can be supercharged with more lifetrons, the clothes you wear can be magnetized with them, etc., etc.

"This simple practice—ATTRACT AND BLESS—enables you to maintain continual CONSCIOUS MENTAL CONTACT with the Lifetronic Power of the universe. Failure to make this contact by lack of awareness and wrong living habits deprives the body of the Lifetronic energy it needs to function properly. We then become ill, until the Lifetronic balance is restored.

Our quiet-mannered Space Friend paused to allow these amazing ideas time to sink into our minds. By now Jim Lindy had found his voice and managed to ask a question:

THIS SIDE FOR STUDENT NOTES

"Will this wonderful practice overcome physical symptoms of Old age and Senility?"

"Old Age and Senility are nothing more than continued chronic ailments due to SUB-OXIDATION (lack of air) of the bloodstream. Air carries life electricity or Lifetrons. When the oxidation capacity of the body cells is decreased due to wrong food and insufficient activity, the entire body ages prematurely. By means of 'A & B' Technique applied to the foods and liquids in your daily meals, an 'overage' – that is, a larger than normal quantity-of proper electronic ionizing Lifetrons can be supplied to your body. No complicated man-made machine or device is required to accomplish this. Your own BODY and MIND are all the equipment you need. Your own FORCE CENTERS of the body can be stimulated by LIFETRONIC ENERGY and speeded up to throw off impurities and waste poisons that impede the flow of life forces. But regular daily practice is essential. Set a certain time of the day for your practice and keep it up no matter how little the results appear to be. Continued practice will increase your ability. It is ever the HALF-HEARTED who fail!"

Our Space Friend looked earnestly at each of us.

"You say wrong foods affect the body's oxidation process? Why Is that?" Jim inquired.

"Most Earthlings, while able to enjoy a great variety of foods, overeat of foods which do not aid oxidation of the body cells. The one food substance which acts roost powerfully as an oxidation catalyst (booster) is usually neglected."

"And that substance is?"

"Green magic, Chlorophyll from living plants. Taken into the body regularly each day, In its natural form as green leaves or raw green vegetable juices freshly pressed, chlorophyll brings MORE AIR—hence more Lifetrons—to every cell. This dynamic natural action benefits humans by vitalizing the body cells and allowing better elimination of their poisons."

Jim and I made a mental note to include a large glassful of green fresh, vegetable juice in our diet daily. For those who are not too familiar with raw vegetable juices, a visit to your local health food store or juice bar will pay big dividends health wise. Most juice bars supply fresh juices of celery, spinach, alfalfa, parsley, watercress, etc. Beginners may prefer a combination of all green juices with a little carrot or fresh

THIS SIDE FOR STUDENT NOTES

tomato Juice added for mildness and extra flavor. "Potassium Mix" this beverage is called.

"Do any other special foods contribute greatly to the vitality of the Venusian people?" I asked.

"Lifetrons, when concentrated in living, growing plants at the earliest stage of their growth, produce a force known as VRIL," replied our instructor. "Sprouted seeds are the most LIVING FOODS Nature has provided. Daily use of sprouts is relatively new to your planet, but the Venusians have used them for many hundreds of Venusian years and consider them quite an ancient custom. They use the 'A & B' Technique on their sprouts before and after sprouting the seeds. Although young growing seeds attract an abundant supply of Lifetrons, we accelerate the process by our minds and increase the VRILLIC content."

"Is VRIL also stored within animals and man?"

"Yes. VRIL is latent within all living creatures. It is stored as a mighty positive force at the base of every creature's spine before birth. In most beings, VRIL remains dormant, unused...in essence, it is ATOMIC POWER...able to destroy like a flash of lightning. Yet, in awakened New Age Man, VRIL is capable of being raised, disciplined into a HEALING FORCE that can instantly invigorate, heal and perfect humanity. On this mightiest of agencies Lon-Zara, Dr. C, and all of our wisest and noblest ones chiefly rely. It is invincible. It permeates all the subtler forces of Nature and is often considered to be that one Original Force or Energy under which the various forms of matter are made manifest. The Brahmins call it 'Fohat!"

"How may we safely awaken such tremendous force?"

"First, learn and practice the paramount science of observing BALANCE in your every thought, feeling and action. Form a positive daily habit of BALANCING the Power Principle (Energy, Strength) with the Love principle (Harmony). Make a vigorous use of the Wisdom Principle to keep your physical, mental and emotional energies in better BALANCE at all times.

This brings greater poise and control. Lacking this control you can never achieve other than imperfect and feeble power over the slumbering VRIL within you. Next, practice faithfully the Lifetronic Atom Cleansing exercise previously revealed to you. INCREASE YOUR AWARENESS OF LIFETRON So Be diligent in your use of the 'A & B' Technique. I have shown you; seek to extend your command over the Lifetrons day

THIS SIDE FOR STUDENT NOTES

by day. Eat Live Foods only. Seek an Upward rather than a downward MODULATION of all your creative energies. At the proper time, the Higher Brothers will unfold the next important step."

Jim and I assured the wise and mysterious messenger that we would apply ourselves whole-heartedly to our New Age practices. Much that had been a mystery to us-the how and why of Dis-Ease, the location and powers of the Life-Switch In Man, the utter futility of "man-made cures", the Health Pyramid Principle, the scavenger virus in meat, the True capstone of Christ Love, the secret of Modulation Upward, the magical Lifetrons—all this and more had been taught to us clearly and simply. Indeed, we owed a debt of everlasting gratitude to our Beloved Venusian Friends. How could we repay them? By re-giving to others.

Still, our immediate joyous feeling could not be contained, and we thanked the messenger profusely for the marvelous assistance he and the Venusian Lon-Zara, and Dr. C, had given at a time of great need. The quiet one smiled and turning to Jim Lindy, said:

"Jim, you have made splendid progress in health. It pleases us to know that your planet has such strong and determined NEW AGE SOULS as you and Michael. Without your positive cooperation our own activities in your behalf would have been hindered. We bless you. We bless all of you who choose to LOOK UP to a better, grander way of LIFE, LOVE and LIGHT. You, Jim, have rebuilt your broken body, gained a keener mind, and increased your higher sensitivity. You are now a NEW AGE EARTHLING. Find a New Age activity that appeals most to the NEW YOU, and put heart and soul into it. Do this, and to you it will never be work. It will be PLAY! And the harder you play, the HEALTHIER you will become!"

The three of us again gazed out from the summit of Mt. Hollywood upon the metropolitan world below. From up here, the great city looked so peaceful, so quiet and inactive. Yet, we knew that under this distant, gentle—seeming exterior there was plenty of bustling, seething activity, not all of it gentle or peaceful; for the forces of Negative was always present.

They had to be wisely controlled, transmuted by the forces of Positive if a happier, healthier level of life was to be shared by man on this planet—this "schoolroom" planet – Earth.

We could now see another party of climbers and several individuals wending their way up the mountain trail. In a moment or two the summit would be crowded.

THIS SIDE FOR STUDENT NOTES

Aware of this, our Venusian visitor bade us farewell. The shock of parting was numbing, intense. His large eyes looked deep into ours for a long moment. No words were spoken, for these beings communicate much more by their feelings and thoughts than by mere words. The power, love and wisdom that flashed from those wondrous eyes...no words of mine are adequate to express.

"Seek Life, Know Life, BE LIFE" was the thought he projected to us in that silent moment. This was followed immediately by another: "Seek Love, Know Love, BE LOVE. Then a third and final: "BALANCE THE TWO...Keep this up unceasingly and it will make you so positively VITAL that health and happiness will reign throughout your whole being."

We began to retrace our steps leading back down the mountainside. He accompanied us only a few yards, and then bade us go on without him. As we did so, he took a side trail in the direction of a more heavily wooded area, and was soon lost to our sight.

I glanced at Jim. He was filled with irrepressible emotions. His intuitive feeling had been correct. It had led him onward and upward to make this contact, and now he too was a Contactee. All his fondest dreams, hopes and ambitions had been realized with a suddenness that seemed almost dazzling.

Yet it was all due simply to the efficient way in which the Space People go about their humanitarian tasks.

Jim's leave of absence was now up, and he was needed up North. His friends there would surely be astonished to see the NEW Jim Lindy. Now sun-bronzed, lithe of figure, he bore no resemblance to the deplorable being that had greeted me so painfully at the L.A. International Airport. Jim's moist eyes met mine. Suddenly he caught my hand in a warm, friendly hand-clasp. It was the strong, earnest grip of a NEW AGE INDIVIDUAL who knew that the Wise Ones had blessed him beyond price.

"Come on Jim," I suggested, "let's find a way to bless the whole human race!"

THE END & THE BEGINNING

THIS SIDE FOR STUDENT NOTES

VENUSIAN

Secret – Science!

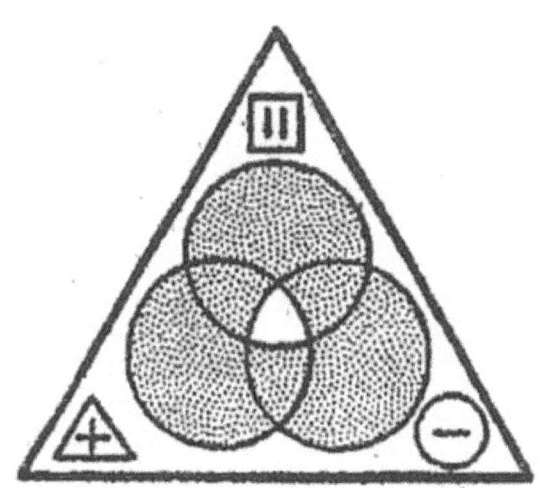

By

Michael X

"VENUSIAN SECRET-SCIENCE"

By MICHAEL X

This is an Educational and Inspirational Course of Study dealing with interplanetary subjects? It is especially written and intended for NEW AGE Individuals everywhere. The following SEVEN lessons are included in this special study:

1. "COMMUNICATING WITH VENUS"
2. "THE COSMIC PLAN REVEALED"
3. "CHOSEN BY THE WISE ONES"
4. "YOUR GRADUATION PROM EARTH"
5. "YOUR MAGIC LIFE ON VENUS"
6. "VENUSIAN SECRET POWERS"
7. "THE BEINGS BEYOND VENUS"

Statements in this Course are based on Scientific and Super-Sensory Findings. No claim is made as to what the information cited may do in any given case and the Publishers assume no obligation for opinions expressed or implied herein by the author.

INNER LIGHT/GLOBAL COMMUNICATIONS © 2008/2017

SPECIAL ATTENTION

YOU, the NEW AGE Individual, having purchased this Course, are known to me. In addition to the unusual and important instruction to be found in the Course Itself, another most valuable service has been bestowed upon you.

YOU have been placed within my personal circle of AURIC PROTECTION and ILLUMINATION. Neither space, time nor distance can hinder this beneficial influence from acting constructively for you and accomplishing its GOOD work in your life. This positive power is effective NOW.

As you study this Course, be conscious of great waves of LIFE, LOVE and LIGHT radiating now from me to you. Visualize the Life wave vibrating as a beautiful azure blue color; the Love wave as radiant rose pink; and the Light wave as a brilliant golden yellow.

These living forces of my AURIC CIRCLE will enfold you henceforth by night and day. Though invisible to ordinary physical sight, these forces are nonetheless real and in time you will come to see them spiritually. Nothing can break this uplifting, revivifying auric connection except disbelief or your personal desire not to have it.

I bless you now with the faith of the Shining Ones, and the healing virtues of God's everlasting LIFE.

LOVE and LIGHT!

MICHAEL X

Seer of the New Age

AUTHOR'S FOREWORD

"**VENUSIAN SECRET-SCIENCE**" is unlike anything you have ever studied before. This is due to the fact that it comes to you from another world, that exceedingly beautiful and mysterious planet VENUS... our own "Sister Planet" and "Evening Star".

As you study this Course, you will discover how my mind gradually became a "channel for communication with advanced VENUSIAN beings so that the SECRET-SCIENCE they had developed could be transmitted to all Earthlings, ready to receive it. This wonderful Science was developed by far wiser beings than I, and is not the result of one or even a dozen brilliant minds. Many THOUSANDS of human minds concentrated together on Venus, under the direction of the Lord Thinkers, to produce a "Super-Science" for the good of all humankind everywhere.

Three basic principles-LIFE, LOVE and LIGHT-are the positive essentials or "foundation" of their wondrous Science. Upon these three principles all of the "super-structure" of their SECRET-SCIENCE was built. When was this GREAT WORK begun? Not yesterday, nor last year, nor even 1,000 years ago.

"VENUSIAN SECRET-SCIENCE" was discovered, formulated and designed into a workable system THIRTY-THREE million years ago, and it has never failed to do the marvelous, things it was intended to do from the very beginning. For this good and noble reason planet Venus has become a POSITIVE world. Those beings fortunate enough to live on Venus at this moment are so ALIVE, so LOVING, and so INTELLIGENT they are far in advance of us Earthlings. Indeed, the people of Venus are among the most ADVANCED beings in this solar system. However, you will be pleased to know that such positive progress is a part of GOD'S PLAN FOR ALL MANKIND everywhere!

This means that in time to come (and that time isn't far off for it IS later than you think!) our own planet Earth will blossom forth with a NEW GOLDEN AGE far surpassing anything Earthman has yet known. But always, the Elders of Venus will be far ahead. They started earlier and as a natural consequence have learned more about GOD'S UNIVERSE and THE COSMIC PLAN.

The Venusians, however, cannot reach down and lift us by our "bootstraps" into a higher consciousness and a restore perfect life. At all times they will. INSPIRE and ENLIGHTEN those who seek their aid, and most of this good work is done by THOUGHT PROJECTION to Earth students who have prepared themselves to receive it.

THIS SIDE FOR STUDENT NOTES

Of course, this is an exceedingly wonderful advantage to sincere NEW AGE men and women. We can, through wise guidance of Cosmic Teachers, speed up our mental and spiritual evolution tremendously!

The Course you are about to study is intended by the Lord Thinkers of Venus to serve as a dynamic stimulus to your TOTAL MIND as well as SOUL. New horizons will be opened up within you with each new lesson, so that your mental vistas will expand and a glorious new REALIZATION of Life, Love and Light will form itself inside your soul.

I recommend that you make it a point to read and re-read the lessons three or more times over a period of the next three months. You will realize best results if you enter into this fascinating study with an open mind', and a positive, constructive view. Many "jewels" of wisdom and much "rare wine" of secret knowledge await you herein; do not let your good elude you by blocking it with doubts or negation of any kind.

In order to increase the benefits and value of this study, each lesson is followed by several questions which those who want to make a thorough study of these teachings should try to answer for themselves after they read the text of the lesson. By doing this, you will become a deeper thinker, will derive greater benefit from these teachings, and be better able to uplift others who have not yet found the HIGHER LIFE.

This Science may at first seem strange to you. That is to be expected. However, the "strangeness" will soon vanish as you become familiar with its marvelous principles and apply them in your own life.

Be diligent, and you will attain. In these pages you and I will TRAVEL TOGETHER on the positive UPWARD PATH leading to the stars. It will be a magnificent adventure. Take my hand and let us begin!

MICHAEL X

THIS SIDE FOR STUDENT NOTES

COMMUNICATING WITH VENUS

Lesson 1

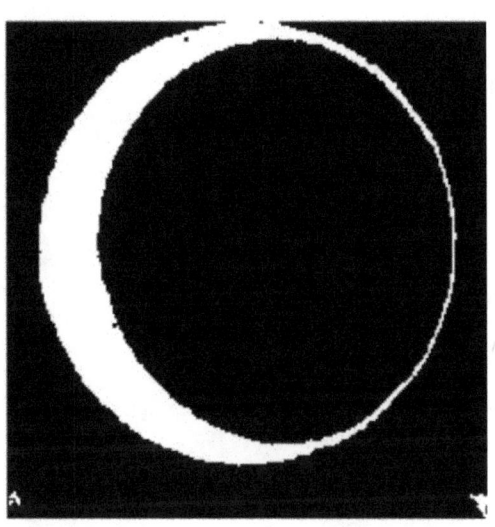

"**IF** you are diligent in your application of New Age truths from now on, you will quite likely reach the COMING MILLENIUM 'in the flesh' and get safely past the Great Shift without the slightest bit of physical harm coming to you during the whole thrilling experience. But you must see to it that the "coverings of the Light" are removed from your mind and spirit. Then you shall know yourself as a true Godlike being, and be ready to take your place in the Age of Peace, Power and Plenty, In the days to come, you will be guided in THE WAY you are to go for your safety and further progress. Much hidden knowledge and valuable instruction will be given you...often in quite strange and, yes, mysterious ways; but always at THE TIME when you need guidance most..."

(From the final page of *FLYING SAUCER REVELATIONS*)

THIS SIDE FOR STUDENT NOTES

Little did I know, when I wrote the above words to you, Just how prophetic they were to become with the passage of time. I could not realize then, that my own mind was destined to act as a CHANNEL for minds far superior to mine.

These new "adventures" began for me shortly after my first successful attempt at "Space Telepathy" in which I had contacted mentally a living human being, a complete stranger to me, who informed me that he was a citizen of planet Venus. The astonishing details of our conversation convinced me of one simple fact. Whoever this mysterious stranger was, he had access to a universal wisdom which the Earth has failed to recognize. Surely a wisdom like this, entrusted to the right people on our own Planet, would prove a great boon to humanity here. And it would aid the higher forces of Venus.

At the conclusion of this first communication, my super-intelligent communicant from Venus gave me definite instructions as to WHEN and HOW I would hear from him again.

"When you next become aware of a certain sound, vibrating in the key of 'D', you will know I am seeking to contact you again, it will be a soft, bell-like note of an unusual, penetrating quality. Watch for it on the morrow, 1 hour after sunset. I shall then explain many seeming mysteries, and banish whatever doubts you may now have regarding me."

With these words our communication ceased and I could hear his voice no longer. I looked closely at my watch and saw that it indicated 3:00 A.M. We had been in "mental rapport" for one hour, yet it seemed like only a few moments.

A confusion of thoughts occupied my mind. Had I been dreaming so vividly as to believe this astounding experience was real or was It possible that some new and great scientific principle, heretofore unknown and unsuspected by Earthlings, had been demonstrated? The more I thought about it, the more baffling it became. Finally, exhausted as I was from tossing this thought about in my mind, a deep and comforting sleep overpowered me and I slept for many hours.

Awakening the following morning from my sleep, I found myself feeling unusually refreshed and invigorated. All of the events of the previous night standing-out clearly in my mind. I have never prided myself on having an exceptionally good memory, yet oddly enough, I could recall with the greatest ease and clarity every word and idea presented to me by my mysterious friend whose dynamic mental waves had reached me from the wondrous and beautiful planet Venus.

THIS SIDE FOR STUDENT NOTES

Immediately, I set to work transcribing on paper all of the important information the "Venusian" had conveyed to me. This was accomplished speedily and entrusted to my loyal Secretary for safekeeping, and perhaps publication later. I now began to realize, more than before, how remarkable were the mental communications I had received. At the same time, I wondered what the being who had conversed with me by "Thought-Transmission" between his world and mine, was really like.

However, a few hours would tell, and though I looked forward with great eagerness to the promised interview that very evening, I busied myself as best I could with the day's work. After all necessary activities of the day had been duly performed, I got into my car and went for a drive to the nearby hills of Santa Barbara. Just in case you might not be familiar with this lovely little city, let me hasten to say that it is one of the most beautiful beach and mountain resort towns in all the world. Industry has not polluted the air of Santa Barbara. It's still fresh and pure and vitalizing, the way the Creator intended it to be.

Few towns on the California coast have developed such a wholesome, peaceful spirit as this one. Good music, all the fine arts and wonderful culture flourish in Santa Barbara. Yes, it's indeed a beautiful town. Fabulous trees, flowers, and lush green vegetation thrive in the semi-tropical climate. For these and other good reasons I settled here some years ago; and to my mind it is still the same wonderful "Garden of Eden" that it was when I first "discovered" it!

As I drove towards the mountains, I had no particular destination in mind except to find as peaceful a spot as possible from which to make my second mental contact with the Venusian. Our next communication by Telethot was scheduled to take place only a half-hour from now. Somehow it seemed to me that the most suitable place for telepathic communication would be some point high in the hills overlooking all of the city. There I could find the essential seclusion and quietude so necessary for success in any telepathic test.

THIS SIDE FOR STUDENT NOTES

At the foot of the hills lies old Santa Barbara Mission— one of a whole chain of such Missions founded by Father Junipero Serra back in the early Spanish days in California. From this famed landmark in Santa Barbara, I turned my car from Los Olivos Avenue onto Mountain Drive. I drove in a relaxed manner, slowly and carefully wending ray way up the mountain road. In a few minutes, "Mountain Drive" branched off into another road called "Los Canoas". This road led up in the direction of a very secluded Monastery owned and built many years ago by the Franciscan Fathers. It was known as "Mount Calvary Retreat House", and had been originally selected by the fathers as an ideal location for long periods of peaceful meditation on the Christian mysteries.

Intuitively then, I sensed that I should continue in the direction of the Retreat House, and that before I got to the summit where the Franciscans were located, the perfect spot for "Telethot" would be found. Los Canoas road led me to a small signpost. It indicated that I should now follow "El Clelito" road, and it would lead me in the direction I wished to go. This I did, and was soon gratified to see an ancient, weather beaten rustic sign pointing towards the Retreat House which was only ½ mile further up the winding mountain road. By this time, the sun had set below the horizon. Quickly I turned onto the small road leading upward, searching carefully as I drove, for the best place to stop. The higher I went, the more beautiful the scenic view became; and the quieter and more ideal the atmosphere seemed.

About 500 yards from the Mount Calvary Retreat House, I came to a natural lookout spot Just off the road. From this vantage point close to the summit of the mountain, one could see the peaceful green valley below. The entire Santa Barbara countryside, beautiful as a dream, stretched out for miles to the south. Above me, like a shimmering silver disk, hung the moon...the brightest planet in the sky. Venus, our "Evening Star" was clearly visible also.

I pulled my car onto the mountain ledge and got out to walk around. This was certainly an ideal spot for mental communication; there were no signs of life for a considerable distance. The view from this height was awe-inspiring, but what impressed me most was the utter stillness here. It was so quiet, as to seem almost "hallowed ground", the serene stillness broken only by occasional sounds of birds. How truly wise the Franciscan monks were to have chosen such a perfect location for their Retreat House.

I climbed onto a large, smooth rock, sat down and looked at my watch. 6:20. I had ten minutes. There was a little time yet to think over the situation. If all went well,

THIS SIDE FOR STUDENT NOTES

another scientific "miracle" was soon to occur. From another world 26,886,000 miles distant, the thought waves of a most extraordinary human being were to contact my mind. A new and illuminating conversation would take place between us that might very well transform my life.

This remarkable being on far away Venus must have some vitally important purpose behind these communications with me. Some grand purpose was undoubtedly being served in this unusual fashion, but as yet it was a mystery. Perhaps with the making of this new contact I'd get an explanation for that mystery and learn the real purpose of my communicant. By nature I am a practical soul, not given to over-credulity, hallucinations, nor somnambulism. However, my previous "conversation" with the Venusian had as much sense of reality to it as any long distance phone call I'd ever received from my personal friends in Los Angeles. Telepathy between Worlds seemed by no means beyond the realm of possibility, and if…

I cut my musing short to glance again at my watch. Time had passed rapidly. It was Six Twenty-eight. Any moment now. All was intensely quiet. Not a sound anywhere around. I relaxed in the warm breezes of the California evening air and looked upwards to the bright and lovely planet Venus. Then I heard it, a pulsing, vibrant musical chord in the key of "D". How beautiful and melodious it was, with an ethereal quality about it that made it strangely different from any musical sound I have ever heard on Earth. It seemed to vibrate with unusual overtones that at once relaxed me in the most wonderful manner. All my tense expectancy vanished and I waited calmly for the voice of the Venusian teacher.

"My greetings to you Michael and to all my Brothers and Sisters on planet Earth!"

His voice was vibrant with an earnest feeling, and every word had a pleasing "Velvet-smooth" quality about it. I felt highly elated. This was the same remarkable personage with whom I had conversed at length in the early hours of the previous day. Now I knew that our communications were real and that Telethot between planets was completely feasible, though I did not yet understand the principles governing it.

I joyously returned the greetings to my Venusian friend. He seemed very pleased to hear my voice. Again he spoke.

"First of all, Michael, I want to thank you for your sincere belief in me and my world. It was your faith in my promise to again contact you this evening that has

THIS SIDE FOR STUDENT NOTES

brought our minds together for this important meeting. You are wondering who I am and what my real purpose is in communicating with an inhabitant of Earth. These are natural questions and I shall answer them now. As I revealed to you in our last conversation, I am a human being similar in basic structure to your people on Earth, with certain modifications as you will discover In due time. I am known on my planet as Lon-Zara, Keeper of the Lifetronic Flame. My special work here has to do with the purifying, healing and rejuvenating of those people of Venus who have not yet attained to a higher state of adept ship. You should know that there are numerous levels of mind here, just as there are on Earth. Yet even the lower grades of mentalities here are remarkable, and would be considered "brilliant" if contrasted to the minds of beings on certain other planets in our solar system.

"My purpose in contacting you tonight by Telethot is two-fold; One, to assure you that we of Venus are Godly people, having discovered some millions of years ago our relationship with the Father-Mother principles of creation in the universe. We have discovered that One Power rules the entire Cosmos and this Power is always Interested in how the human race is progressing in its divine unfoldment. We serve the higher interests of your planet as well as our own. Some of our people are living on Earth now, yet they have seldom been recognized as being anything other than your own fellow Earthlings...Our mission is to provide an 'awakening stimulus' of a spiritual nature to the minds of those whom we contact, and to direct them onto THE PATH. But I don't want to confuse you with too many details so soon. Simply put, my purpose is to unfold to you and to all your sincere friends and students on Earth, the basic truths of our 'SECRET-SCIENCE' of Life, Love and Light. This great knowledge will not be given to you all at once. Each time we are in 'mental communion' you shall have increased in understanding, so that more of the 'Science' can be transmitted to your mind and soul. At the proper time, when we are sure you can handle and direct certain unusual forces within you, you will be entrusted with SOUL-POWERS as yet undreamed of by your people.

"These powers, used by higher-minded Earthlings, shall serve to usher in the COMING GOLDEN AGE wherein your Planet shall blossom forth at last with startling new SPIRITUAL powers that will inaugurate the regime of enlightened SOULS.

"My second purpose in contacting you is to reveal to you the working principles of Telethot (MENTAL RADIO) and of Menta-Vision (MENTAL TELEVISION) in order that our future mental communications shall be more perfect and enjoyable. On Venus, the science of telepathy long since has superseded all other means of 'Thought

THIS SIDE FOR STUDENT NOTES

Communication', and has become so simple and & commonplace that other methods now seem crude.

At this point in our SOUL EVOLUTION we are born with positive telepathic powers. We inherit telepathy now, just as earthmen inherit a particular temperament or character or physical prowess. It is easier and more effective for us to PROJECT THOUGHTS than it is to speak words.

"Therefore, while many of us can and do speak audibly, we consider it a backward step and prefer to use the natural faculty of Telethot and the power of Menta-Vision by which it is possible for intelligent human beings to 'commune' with one another on every humanized planet in our solar system."

At this point Lon-Zara paused, sensing my question. I had in mind asking him HOW the human brain operates so as to make such amazing transmission of thoughts a reality. However, to ray astonishment, my Cosmic Teacher (for such I now realized was true) answered me before I had even consciously framed my question into a complete idea.

"TWO Primal forces exist in the universe." he said. "In total aspect they make up THE ONE POWER that runs all of the Cosmos, and animates all the intelligent beings therein. One of these forces is known as VITICITY, the other is known as ELECTRICITY. Scientists on earth are familiar with this second force, but are totally unaware of the existence of a first force: VITICITY. Whereas Electricity is an expression of PHYSICAL energy, the force of Viticity is an expression of MENTAL energy. One is the power of matter and the other is the power of MIND. Which of these two is superior?"

"Viticity, or the power of MIND is superior," I answered at once. "I have always believed that intelligence has supremacy over matter, and can mold it to any desired purpose. In fact, we have a commonly recognized saying on Earth to the effect that psychic phenomena are due to "Mind over Matter!"

"That is indeed true," said Lon-Zara. "It is MENTAL POWER that rules the entire universe; and it is this same unsuspected force of Viticity that is utilized by us to TRANSMIT OUR THOUGHT IMAGES through vast reaches of space to any human being anywhere in the universe! Space and distance offer no barriers to the dynamic power of Viticity. It is essential, however, that the person who wishes to 'receive' Telepathic messages be able to 'attune' himself (or herself) to the proper mental wavelength. Also, the intensity of vitical power used in 'transmitting' one's thought is

THIS SIDE FOR STUDENT NOTES

very important. In order to make these vital points much clearer to you, I shall now project from my brain into yours, a larger VOLTAGE of VITRONS, These 'vitrons' are tiny units of vitical force. A vitron is opposite in polarity to an electron which as you know, is a tiny unit of electrical force. Notice the effect."

A split second later, an astounding thing happened. I began to SEE with my "inner eye" in a most vivid manner, and in FULL COLOR! Before, only ray psychic faculty of "distant hearing" had been actively functioning for me, NOW I could see and study whatever scenes came into my mental focus. At this moment I could not get a view of my Teacher Lon-Zara. Evidently he was not yet ready to show himself. I consoled myself by thinking that very soon I might have the privilege of seeing him; and with my hopes high began to observe the IMAGE that was now appearing on my "mental screen." I found it most unusual and enlightening.

"I see a diagram of the inner workings of a human brain." I remarked as soon as I was calm enough to continue. "It reveals the position and function of man. Pituitary and pineal glands, the PSYCHIC organs used for Telethot and Menta-Vision."

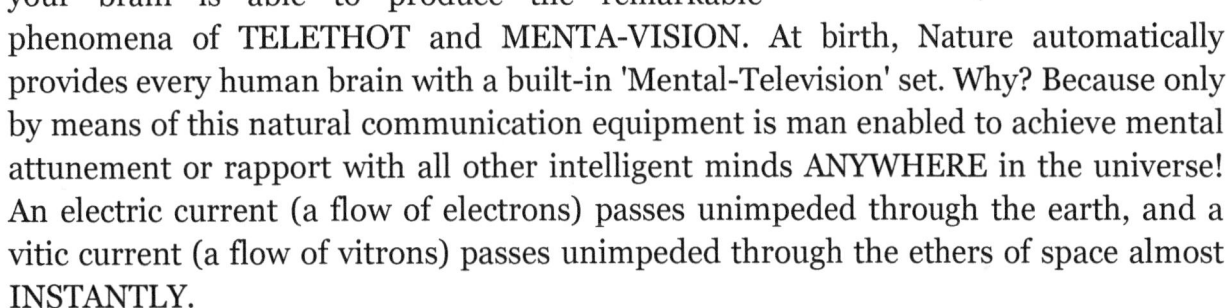

Lon-Zara was pleased, "Splendid!" he said. "Now if you will follow the diagram as I direct, (see Diagram No. 1) I shall reveal to you exactly HOW your brain is able to produce the remarkable phenomena of TELETHOT and MENTA-VISION. At birth, Nature automatically provides every human brain with a built-in 'Mental-Television' set. Why? Because only by means of this natural communication equipment is man enabled to achieve mental attunement or rapport with all other intelligent minds ANYWHERE in the universe! An electric current (a flow of electrons) passes unimpeded through the earth, and a vitic current (a flow of vitrons) passes unimpeded through the ethers of space almost INSTANTLY.

"This wonderful faculty for 2-way THOUGHT COMMUNICATION is truly one of the greatest gifts God bestowed upon Man. Of course, just as with any of man's other faculties, the power must be developed by active exercise if it is expected to be of the greatest service and value to him. TELETHOT and MENTA-VISION are New Age faculties that will open up glorious new vistas for those Earthlings who will develop

THIS SIDE FOR STUDENT NOTES

them. Ignorance will be forever banished, for with these faculties all beings are capable of SEEING, HEARING and TALKING to one another via "Mental Television." This means that mental communion of mind to mind, from planet to planet (Earth to Venus, Venus to Earth, etc.) from Teacher to Pupil irrespective of space or distance, is not only being accomplished NOW but will be a REALITY for many more sincere Earthlings in the New Age, the GOLDEN MILLENIUM just ahead!

"In the Diagram, (small figure 1) indicates your THOUGHT RECEIVER, or in anatomical terms, the Pituitary gland. This is the contact point within your physical brain that enables you to RECEIVE the thought-waves of others from any distant point on Earth or from some other inhabited planet. Figure 2 in the diagram designates your 'Vitronic' or THOUGHT PICTURE SCREEN. It consists of optic nerve cells especially designed for forming mental images. When this area of nerve cells is energized during sleep you have DREAMS, usually in black and white and sometimes in full color. Now we come to the third essential part of your built-in 'TV set', namely the THOUGHT TRANSMITTER. This is your Pineal Gland (figure 3). It is the positive contact point whereas the Pituitary gland is the negative contact point or "terminal".

"Figure 4 shows the cerebellum, which is the main organ of the Subconscious mind. Notice how the small arrows, indicating VITRONS, flow upward and across to the Pineal gland, then into the 'Picture Screen' thereby energizing it. Some of the tiny vitrons flow into the Pituitary gland where the Ego or Self of the individual resides. The self then interprets the MENTAL IMAGES created by the vitrons, as specific visual messages complete with COLOR, SOUND, and other sensory stimuli. Notice how vitrons follow a path into the MENTAL TV SET through the cerebellum (Subconscious) and complete a 'circuit' by flowing out through the cord of the cerebrum (fig. 5) or Conscious mind. Venusians have discovered that the more VITRONS one is able to 'store up' or accumulate within the cerebellum or Subconscious organ of the brain, the easier one can TRANSMIT thought images through space. TELETHOT requires much fewer vitrons than does MENTA-VISION.

"I shall now give you FIVE simple rules that will aid you in perfecting yourself MENTALLY so that you will be able to receive further communications from me telepathically with even greater ease and effectiveness.

"RULE 1. To send or receive mental messages, the most important step is to learn to consciously RELAX so that your Conscious mind does not hinder nor interrupt the process of attunement. 10 Or 15 minutes before attempting to send or receive telepathically, assume a position of physical relaxation in a comfortable chair.

THIS SIDE FOR STUDENT NOTES

You should be in a secluded place where you are not likely to be disturbed. You may then close your eyes and breathe deeply and exhale slowly until a peaceful, soothing state is experienced. Do not, however, allow yourself to go to sleep. You want to be near the sleep state but still consciously aware. Midway between your Conscious mind and your Subconscious mind is a balance or 'neutral zone' wherein you are consciously in HARMONY with the activities of your Subconscious. This area or neutral zone in which the Conscious and Subconscious minds act together is known as the SUBLIMINAL STATE. This must never be confused with the 'unconscious state', nor with the 'trance state'. It is more like a deep REVERIE wherein your Conscious mind is NOT UNCONSCIOUS, BUT IS SO CONCENTRATED upon the disclosures being made to it by the Subconscious mind as to be oblivious, at least partially, to its immediate surroundings. In this SUBLIMINAL STATE, your Conscious mind may enter into and become attuned in VITIC vibration with the mind of another person on Earth or on another Planet, and thus acquire KNOWLEDGE from the Subconscious mind or Intellect of that other individuality. Practice then, entering the SUBLIMINAL STATE.

"RULE 2. After entering the subliminal state, maintain it throughout the process of telepathic communication. A Lapis Linguis or Telolith psychic gem should be held in your hand as an aid in 'stepping up' the psychic attunement of your mind and body. It will also serve to focalize and intensify the higher thought vibrations you are seeking to contact; and this will keep your Conscious mind from descending below the SUBLIMINAL STATE into the 'trance' or 'somnambulant' state. In due time, none of these physical aids will be necessary either to enter or sustain the desired state, for your mind will grow more skilled In telepathic work through dally practice. The performance of Telethot is a 'mastered science' to men and women on Venus, but is still a new and strange art to Earthlings. Therefore practice is most essential to you.

"RULE 3- Arrange definite times to send and receive telepathic messages among one or more close friends, who are sympathetic and understanding. Persons who are close to you in affection and who like to cooperate with you, are best. Be careful who you talk to about these matters. Although the faculty of Telethot is now gaining recognition by your scientists of Earth, there are still many people who scoff at it through ignorance. Their ridicule might lower your self- confidence so it is wisest to go about this vital practice as quietly and as carefully as you can. As to the best hours for practicing Telethot, the quiet hours of night or just after daybreak are best. People are most relaxed at these hours hence are most impressionable telepathically.

THIS SIDE FOR STUDENT NOTES

"RULE 4, To TRANSMIT your mental-messages to another, it is essential first to 'fix' your Conscious mind earnestly upon the particular person (either upon the Earth or Venus) with whom the mental correspondence is desired. Also try to mentally see or VISUALIZE him in his usual environment. The secret here is to form in your mind a large hollow tube or tunnel and picture the other person as appearing at the far end of the tube while you are at this end. Now formulate your thought with as much precision and definiteness as possible. It will help at first if you will write down a simple message clearly and have it in sight to refer to. The name of the person you are sending your thought to, should be used freely to 'attract' his attention. Immediately after his attention has been attracted and mental attunement achieved, you will at once recognize the attunement by a peculiar mental reaction. You will feel 'connected' mentally. It sometimes happens that a vivid mental picture of the person is seen, and the sound of his voice heard distinctly. These are real phenomena of the mental senses and become more pronounced as you awaken these long dormant faculties. As you sit facing the other person, focus your attention just above and between his eyes. His 'receiver' or Pituitary gland is located at that point. Assume a positive, affirmative state of mind and speak the words you wish him to hear. Visualize each word as traveling from your 'transmitter'(Pineal) down the hollow tube to the receiver. Emotionalize each word by seeing it AFLAME WITH BLUE FIRE as it leaves your mind. The more vivid you make your message the more vital it will be.

"RULE 5- To RECEIVE telepathic communications, you are to drop the positive and directing attitude which is required for 'thought transmission', and should instead adopt a passive and receptive state, with the SUBLIMINAL-mind acutely sensitive. In this condition, not only will your clairaudient sense of hearing (Mental Radio) begin to function more clearly and distinctly; but frequently the clairvoyant sense of inner sight (Mental TV) will momentarily become activated, causing you to see an actual physical 'image' of the person you are communicating with. It is a good idea to jot down all words, sentences and messages that come to you, in a private notebook as soon as you receive them. Do this as soon as you return from the subliminal to the fully conscious state of awareness.

"And now I bid you put these five rules into practice at once, so that during the next week you will have prepared yourself mentally, to sustain longer M conversations by Telethot with me, one week hence at the location where you now are, and at the same hour. I shall then unfold to you many, more fascinating secrets of our universal science. Till then, Michael X, may Life, Love and Light be with you!"

THIS SIDE FOR STUDENT NOTES

VENUSIAN HEALTH SCIENCE & VENUSIAN SECRET SCIENCE

SPECIAL NOTE: The theme of this first lesson suggests the following important questions:

1. What are the two reasons why Lon-Zara wished to contact Michael X? State briefly.

2. Why do you think vocal speech between human beings is considered a "backward step" by the Venusians?

3. Which of the TWO primal forces – Electricity or Viticity – is the superior force?

4. Which primal force is used to transmit thoughts?

5. Why does Mother Nature equip every human being at birth with a built-in "Mental Television set"?

6. What is the name given to the "neutral zone" midway between the Conscious mind and the Subconscious mind?

THIS SIDE FOR STUDENT NOTES

THE COSMIC PLAN REVEALED
Lesson 2

I did not hear from Lon-Zara again until a full week had elapsed. However, I made use of every chance I could get during this time to practice the FIVE RULES of mental communication according to the instructions given me. All my close friends were "enlisted" to aid me in my various experiments at sending and receiving thought vibrations. Use of the Telolith (psychic gem) helped us to transmit stronger vibrations and also pick up vibrations more quickly. We made the whole thing as much of a "game" as possible, and I believe this feeling of enjoyment increased our sense of confidence and satisfaction. All of us noted a definite increase in our telepathic powers by the time Sunday had rolled around.

Sunday morning I rested and conserved my mental energy for the next "interplanetary conversation" with my Venusian teacher later in the evening. There were so many important questions to ask him about, so many long-hidden mysteries X wished to understand. Did the wise beings of Venus really know the answers to Life's puzzles? Did they discover keys to knowledge which have long been veiled from Earthlings? Could this knowledge, if they cared to reveal it, be used by men and women on Earth to transform themselves and thereby assist the higher evolution of the human race?

Of one thing X was certain. Lon-Zara was no ordinary being. A vast intelligence of an extremely high order was his to direct upon any subject of either a mundane or super-mundane nature. I determined that if man be permitted by the higher powers to learn all the answers, surely Lon-Zara, with his advanced mental powers would have gained knowledge of THE COSMIC PLAN of the universe. He would surely know why mankind is embodied in physical form on various planets, and what the purpose of

THIS SIDE FOR STUDENT NOTES

man really is, where he is going and most important...HOW to successfully arrive there.

Thinking along this line, I walked over to my library bookcase and passed my hand idly over the many esoteric volumes I've collected over the years. Intention was not to do any heavy reading, but merely browse through the books in hopes of uncovering something of especial inspirational value to put me in the proper mental vibration for my evening telepathic visit with Lon-Zara. Strangely enough, none of the books held much appeal to me, for the first time in a long while. I decided to replace the books in the case and go for a long walk. Then I noticed the object on the floor. It was a sheet of paper, quite yellowed by age. Oddly, I did not notice it before. It must have fallen out of one of the old books I've purchased recently at one of the Occult Book stores in town. Quickly I reached down, picked up the sheet of paper and was pleased to discover that it contained a typewritten poem, entitled:

LIFE'S PURPOSE

"Forth from planet unto planet

You have gone and you will go.

Space is vast, but we must span it For Life's Purpose is to KNOW.

Earth retains you but a minute;

Make the best of what lies in it Light the pathway where you are.

There is nothing worth the doing that will leave regret or ruing,

As you speed from star to star.

You are part of the beginning,

You are parcel of today;

When he set his worlds to spinning You were flung upon your way.

When this system falls to pieces,

When this pulsing epoch ceases When the 'is' becomes the 'was',

You will live, for you will enter In the Great Creative Center,
in the All-Enduring Cause!"

THIS SIDE FOR STUDENT NOTES

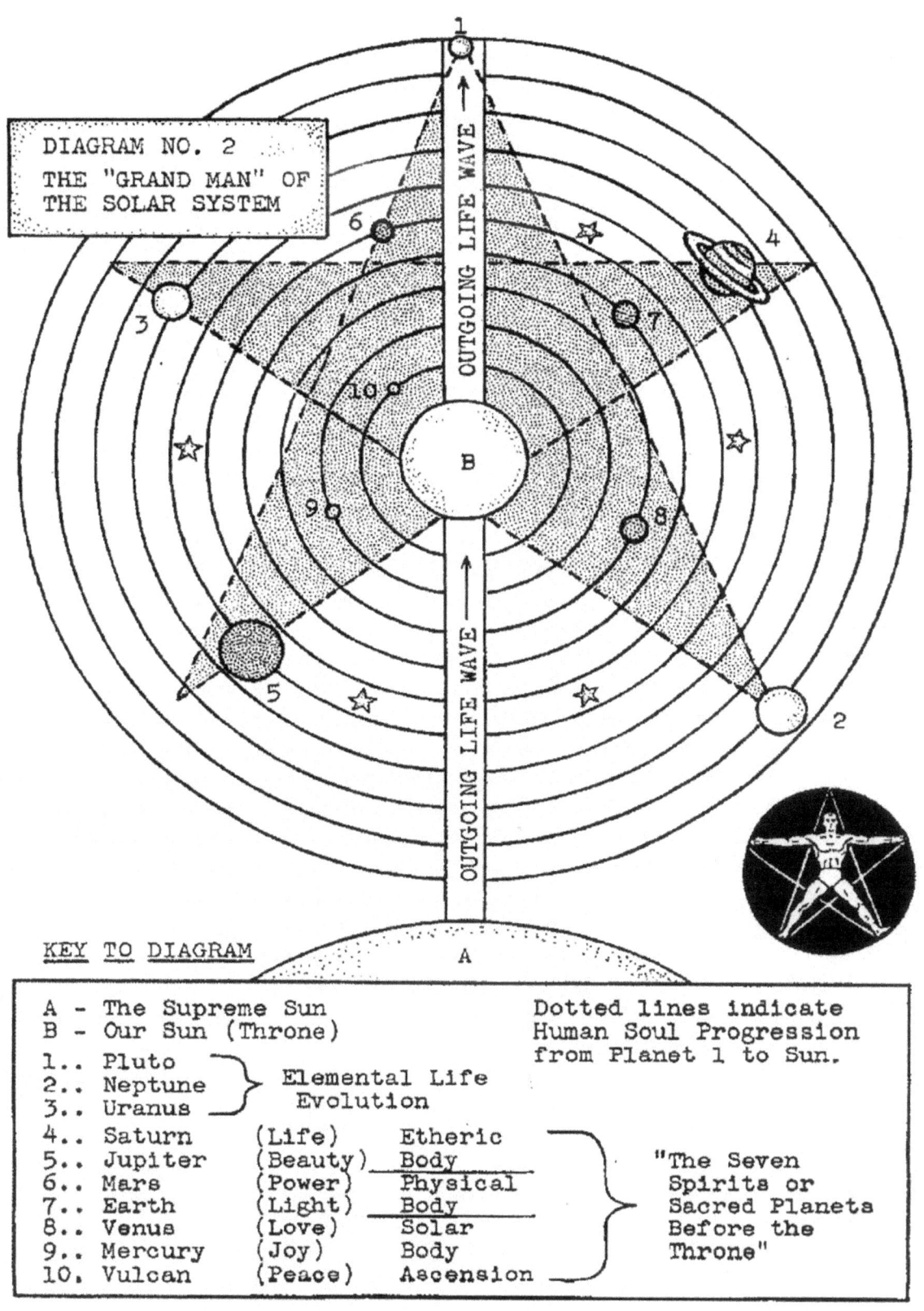

THIS SIDE FOR STUDENT NOTES

At the bottom of the page I read that the poem had been "dictated from the other side of life" by the wonderful and loving soul of Ella Wheeler Wilcox, and taken down by Bessie Warren in Chicago, Illinois.

The more I read the poem over the more it revealed to me. Here was a tremendous spiritual revelation of MAN'S COSMIC JOURNEY stating clearly that you and I and all mankind have gone "forth from planet unto planet" in this Solar System.

So far in our Journey we have reached planet Earth. But where did we start from? And how did we find our way to this particular world? What planet do we go to next? How can we be sure of getting there "on time" as it were? These were some of the vital questions that immediately flashed into my mind as I pondered over the poem. Trusting that my Cosmic Teacher Lon-Zara, would shed new light on these important matters at our next appointment, I glanced at my watch for the time.

Five forty-five. Time to be on my way.

I drove to the same location near Mount Calvary Retreat House, where Lon-Zara had previously contacted me by mental telepathy. It was as quiet and peaceful as ever, and not a disturbing element anywhere in the vicinity. Wonderful! Ten brief minutes to relax myself, and once again I would have the great Joy of conversing with a living, thinking, highly intelligent human being who was millions of miles distant.

I looked forward to this next communication with Lon-Zara, and with good reason. He radiated such a positive, uplifting spirit of love it was like a "healing treatment" just to be in the presence of his vibrations. Few Earthlings have ever developed love to this positive degree; and those who have truly discovered and demonstrated the power of the heart as a spiritual force in man are on THE PATH to immortal heights.

Lon-Zara's signal came softly but with powerful insistence. The same exquisite chord in the key of "D". It flooded through my being like sunlight through an open doorway.

"Good evening Michael X!" came the clear velvet-soft voice of the Venusian teacher. "It is good to be with you again mentally, even though we are separated physically by a great gulf between your planet and Venus. However, if you remain steadfast and devoted in your attention to the instructions that shall be given you from now on, you shall be taught how to overcome the seeming barrier of space in several other ways. I perceive that the light within your "mental television set" is glowing

THIS SIDE FOR STUDENT NOTES

brighter tonight. That is an indication of progress, showing that your brain is now magnetizing and utilizing more vitrons than formerly. This progress will continue, until a time in the very near future when you will be able to see clearly at any distance. You will then have your clairvoyant power under full voluntary control at all times. Until that stage of development is reached by you, I shall assist from time to time by sending a larger supply of vitrons from my brain to yours.

"Thank you kindly, my wondrous friend," I replied with deep feeling and appreciation. "Already you have helped me to unfold ray telepathic powers by your extraordinary teachings and example, and I am indeed grateful. You have a most effective way of teaching. Simple, practical and to-the- point, yet presented always with understanding and love so that I feel imbued with the confidence, courage and strength to master even greater secrets of the universe!"

I was about to mention the poem I had found, but did not have to. Lon-Zara had read my mind. He spoke quietly.

"That poem, *'Life's Purpose'*, which you found today under rather mysterious circumstances, was directed to you for a special reason by the Lord Thinkers of Venus. It was a most effective means of stimulating your mind in regard to THE COSMIC PLAN. It raised questions in your mind which must be answered in order that you and your loyal friends may enter into a new state of consciousness and an ampler state of being. Then you shall be able to grasp the secret principles of LIFE, LOVE and LIGHT whereby all former limitations will speedily pass away as if they never existed, and you will know at last something of your glorious destiny.

As Lon-Zara said these words, I suddenly felt a tremendous wave of vitrons surge into my body and through my brain. The sensation was powerful, dramatic, intense. Yet I was at the same time aware of an exceedingly blissful, peaceful emotion that was harmonious and delightful. My own "Mental TV Set" had been energized into activity by the amazing mental force of a being some twenty-six million miles away! Once again a picture flashed into focus before my mental vision.

YOUR MARVELOUS COSMIC JOURNEY

"This new Diagram you now see on your Mental Screen is a representation of the great solar system in which you and I are now citizens," Lon-Zara explained, (see Diagram No. 2 on page 101) "We on Venus have learned things about this solar system, its

THIS SIDE FOR STUDENT NOTES

planets and inhabitants that may well seem unbelievable to you, nevertheless what I am about to relate is true in principle. The story we have to tell began eons ago. You are not asked to believe, only try to understand. That is the important thing. And in order that you may more easily comprehend this great story. I shall tell you about yourself, where you first began your 'Cosmic Journey' and how you reached planet Earth where you are now living. As I unfold this story gradually, you will soon perceive the WHY of human life and the definite pattern of your own life.

"If you will now follow the Diagram closely," my Venusian master said, "and proceed with me planet by planet as I outline, we shall make a mental tour of our solar system and, as we progress with this story please feel free to ask me any questions that may come to your mind. With a subject so vast as this, I am sure you will have many good questions. I may not have time to answer all your questions in full detail, for as you can realize we have much SPACE to span during this brief lesson. Certain details can be added to your mind later on, after you have learned the main points."

Seeing that I was eager to begin "traversing the solar system" with him mentally, Lon-Zara began his story.

"Eons ago, long before our solar system was born, the Supreme Mind or Father God who dwells upon the Supreme Sun (See "A" in Diagram) at the center of the Universe, decided to manifest Himself in many life levels within His universe. One of these manifestations was in the form of living beings, a higher form of which was the HUMAN BEING or MAN.

"Man, however, (this includes both sexes) could not be evolved suddenly and without some grand pattern that would assure his development in a definite and positive manner. In order to provide a "perfect pattern" for Man, the Supreme Mind first created a great planetary system, we call it a solar system, out of the Cosmic Dust (electrons) in space, He called this creation the GRAND MAN because it is actually the original pattern for the development of our own physical human bodies! (See Diagram 2, page 101)

"An ancient law tells us, 'As Above, So Below'. We see how this law applies here, for the solar system or GRAND MAN contains seven great planetary powers. Thus it is called the MACROCOSM or large Universe. In the case of Man, we find that his body contains seven principles which correspond perfectly to the qualities built into the seven planets. Of course this is true on a miniature scale so Man is considered to be

THIS SIDE FOR STUDENT NOTES

the MICROCOSM or small universe, with access to all seven of the COSMIC QUALITIES represented by...the seven Sacred Planets of the ancients."

THE SEVEN COSMIC QUALITIES

"Master," I said, "Would you list those seven QUALITIES so I may remember them?"

"The QUALITIES are listed on the Diagram," Lon-Zara replied, "but it will do no harm to impress them upon your mind by repeating them here. They are: (1) Life, (2) Beauty, (3) Power, (4) Light, (5) Love, (6) Joy, and the final and seventh Quality - (7) Peace.

"Then," I concluded, "Man is in reality a Seven-Fold being, living in a Seven-Fold planetary system for the purpose of unfolding each of the Seven Cosmic Qualities?"

"Yes," answered the Venusian, "these are Qualities of the Divine Spark or Spirit that is in you. Your Great Cosmic Journey from Planet to Planet gives you an opportunity to build all seven spiritual qualities into your soul."

Calling my attention once more to the Supreme Sun (A), as shown on the Diagram, he continued. "Your Cosmic Journey began originally at 'A', where you were sent forth on the Outgoing Life Wave as a spiritual spark or 'virgin spirit'. By this term, 'virgin spirit', is meant simply that you did not as yet have any consciousness of 'matter'. In fact, you were then in a state of dreamless sleep, having no 'self-conscious awareness' of any kind. To gain a state of 'waking consciousness' so that you would consciously REALIZE the virtue of all seven Cosmic Qualities and learn to embody them in a SOUL and in a PHYSICAL BODY, was the reason for your Journey. The awakening of this soul within one's self is supremely important.

"On the Outgoing Life Wave you, together with several billion other virgin spirits, quickly reached the lesser Sun of this solar system, ('B') As you will notice by observing the 'KEY' to the Diagram our Sun is referred to as the throne. The seven planets indicated with a gray tint in the Diagram, are called the 'Seven Spirits before the Throne'. These seven planets are, Vulcan, Mercury, Venus, Earth, Mars, Jupiter and Saturn."

"Why are planets 1, 2 & 3 (Pluto, Neptune and Uranus) not included with the other seven?" I asked.

THIS SIDE FOR STUDENT NOTES

"These three planets serve to evolve life in its three elemental or primary stages only," Lon-Zara explained. "The self-conscious or higher stages of Human evolution take place on planets 4, 5, 6, 7, 8, 9 and 10. There are other Planets on the far edge of the Solar System. These Planets serve as the unknown Spiritual 'Incubator' of intelligence. After the soul completes its 'growth' on these unseen Planets, the Solar Logos or Lord of our lesser Sun, relays the Outgoing Life Wave to Planet 1 and its five moons. This is the beginning of your life in matter. However, it was a very simple form of life for you were not yet ready to build a complex body in which to function.

PROGRESSION FROM PLANET TO PLANET

"In due time your spirit progressed to Planet 2, Neptune. There you learned to build a new life form better than the one you had on Planet 1. It was not a complex human form, but you were gaining valuable 'basic training', and would soon be fully prepared to build your human etheric body. On Planet 3, Uranus, you successfully completed your evolution in elementary life forms and were now ready for advancement to beautiful and radiant Saturn, which is Planet 4.

"Then," I said, "according to the COSMIC PLAN we would find no human beings living on Uranus, Neptune and Pluto?"

"There are no people from your particular Life Wave in human form on those three planets," replied the Venusian.

"You must realize, however, that a great number of different Life Waves have been sent out from the Supreme Sun, and it is true that those beings of an advanced Life Wave are able to travel to any planet in our solar system if they so wish. The wise ones do not choose to remain on such planets, for the simple reason that human life is vastly superior and infinitely more desirable on the more ADVANCED worlds."

"How is such interplanetary travel accomplished?" I inquired. "That is, must an advanced human being use a SPACE SHIP of some kind in order to transport his physical body to another planet?"

"Fortunately for Man, the sphere of the mind of each individual reaches to the stars and beyond. It reaches as far as his or her power of PERCEPTION reaches. We on the planet Venus, for example, by the exercise of our clairvoyant and clairaudient powers, may at any moment know what is going on in another world such as Earth. And, if we desire to come into personal contact with it, we leave our physical forms on

THIS SIDE FOR STUDENT NOTES

Venus and go out in our etheric bodies. If we desire to take our physical forms with us to your planet or another, then a third method of travel is employed. That is, space travel by flying discs, or other kinds of spacecraft. Often we hover in a disc near the Earth, and descend unseen in our etheric forms. We visit whomsoever we want, and witness everything without our presence being perceived. We visit the statesman, the minister, the philosopher and writer; we infuse our thoughts into their minds which are useful, and they do not know from whence those thoughts come. If their fixed opinions and prejudices are very strong, they may reject our thoughts; but if they are reasonable people and know how to discriminate, they will follow the silent advice and profit by it. Many a problem of Earth has been solved in this manner and in the near future of Earth many more will be solved.

"It is true," Lon-Zara continued, "that by setting a great amount of will-power into motion we might handle mankind as if they were merely automatons, and we could cause them to do what we please, while they would still imagine that they were following their own inclinations. But to do so would be against the rules of our planet and against the great Law, for the latter decides that each man shall be the creator of his own Karma, or destiny. We are permitted to advise the people and give instruction as we are doing now, but we are not permitted to interfere with their freedom."

Lon-Zara again called my attention to the Diagram. "When you, as a progressive spirit, advanced to the planet Saturn with others of your same Life Wave, you began to build for yourself a new and highly complex form of body. It was an etheric astral body of a human being. This was also known as your 'SOUL BODY'. By this time you had awakened from your dreamless sleep state. You began to dream and picture vividly the physical like you longed to become a part of in order to complete your Cosmic Journey and learn the lessons of all the planets.

"After a long time on Planet 4, you traveled in your astral body to Planet 5 – Jupiter. On this largest and most electrified planet in our solar system (except for the Sun Itself) you brought the development of your Soul Body to the most perfect condition for entering into the next necessary condition of life, namely, self-conscious awareness in a dense PHYSICAL BODY! This great event was to occur on Planet 6, which as you will see, is the world you call MARS. When you awoke for the first time on Mars, in a physical body, the half-way point in your Cosmic Journey had been reached. The planet Mars gave you your first experience in a human physical body, and the body you built for yourself was quite strong and vigorous. Since the predominating quality of Mars is power, primarily of a physical type, the people of

THIS SIDE FOR STUDENT NOTES

Mars are physically very strong. They are great builders, and excel in engineering. Conditions on Mars are nearly identical with those of the Earth, and they are equally as favorable for material human life. All of the fertile plains and valleys of Mars are highly cultivated and thickly populated. Its vast system of ocean-lanes and great cities teem with commerce, and all the human pursuits and occupations which are' common to the Earth prevail also upon Mars.

"But human life on Mars has little or no spiritual quality to it. For this reason, neither you nor your friends would wish to become a part of Martian life again. It would be very much like going back to see the place where you lived when you were a child. It is never quite the same, because YOU are not quite the same individual. You've evolved, grown up and out of that old life. True, it was a wonderful 'stepping stone' to assist you in reaching the place where you are today. But the purpose behind it all was to enable you to go onward, upward and reach a yet higher place tomorrow.

THE PATHS OF PURSUIT AND RETURN

"Under the natural laws which pertain to the solar system, the planet Mars is the kindergarten of human thought and knowledge. The planet Earth is the physical heaven of Mars and the next advanced sphere of life; although Earth itself is but a primary grade in the great University1 for human education. The planet Venus is the physical heaven of Earth, and the next higher succeeding grade in human advancement and progress. On the Earth (Planet 7) you first began the true awakening from your SOUL-SLEEP, by acquiring more 'light' or knowledge about the other and most important side of your nature, the spiritual self. Of course, the vast majority of Earthlings, those of the 'Mass-Minded' who are coming to the Earth for the very first time through a process of re-incarnation from Mars, are traveling the One Path of Pursuit. This means they are exceedingly busy pursuing the external knowledge that is gained by all kinds of STIMULATION of the five physical senses. This gives them knowledge of OUTER things."

"And the other Path," I inquired eagerly, "the Path of Return; who are traveling this Path and to what purpose?"

"New Age individuals of all ages, in all walks of life who are now actively seeking to KNOW THEMSELVES and their real relation to COSMIC LAW, and who have come to realize that the attainment of WISDOM is above mere getting', are the ones on the Path of Return. They are the 'old souls' who have gone through many cycles of rebirth

THIS SIDE FOR STUDENT NOTES

on Mars, then graduated from Mars to the Earth, and have reincarnated in new physical bodies on Earth a sufficient number of times to have gained a great wealth of experience in physical life. Gradually they have converted that experience into WISDOM. Hence, the next planet they will advance to on their Cosmic Journey is Venus (Planet 8). Here, the predominating influence you will feel is the vibration of LOVE, not the love that is known on Mars nor even upon the Earth, but a spiritual force that will lift you to such a hew and high level of consciousness as to enable you to reach your final goal much more swiftly.

"That goal," Lon-Zara said, "is to advance planet by planet from Venus to Mercury (Planet 9) and then to Vulcan (Planet 10) and thence to 'B', where you shall live upon the Sun itself. Yes, our Sun is a 'College in the University of Stars' and is inhabited by the greatest beings in this solar system. They have no dense physical body, but possess a body constructed of what we call 'permanent atoms'. From these special atoms each being builds a SOLAR BODY capable of withstanding light vibrations thousands of times stronger than the brightest sunlight you have ever felt on the Earth. As you will see by the Diagram, humanity generally begins building the SOLAR BODY during incarnation on Venus, though some advanced Earthlings have begun the task while on the Earth. Sanat Kumara and several other great Lords of Venus completed their Solar Bodies during their life on Venus, and by doing so they became radiant, shining beings of mighty power. This took place millions of years ago, and is the real reason why our planet is called 'The Home of the Gods'. More commonly, an individual begins his Solar Body on Venus, continues the good work on Mercury, and finally perfects the Solar Body during his life on Vulcan. Then the ASCENSION is made in the glorious Solar Body to man's home on the SUN.

"Later on," my Venusian master concluded, "you shall learn why and how human life in the 'individualized solar body1 is possible, and why the building of your Solar Body or 'Golden Wedding Garment1 is so essential to your higher progress in this and other solar systems. Now, beloved brother, good night...be at this same place tomorrow evening at 6:30 o'clock for further instruction and a pleasant surprise. Till then, my blessings to you and may you unfold in true wisdom!"

******

SPECIAL PRACTICE: Commit to memory the Diagram on page and from memory, draw the Grand Man. Be sure to show the name and number of each of the Seven Sacred Planets (4 through 10) according to man's progression.

THIS SIDE FOR STUDENT NOTES

CHOSEN BY THE WISE ONES
Lesson 3

IT was late in the afternoon. The sun, in a final burst of glorious orange color, was about to disappear once again behind the Santa Barbara hills. I looked longingly at the brilliant orb as if seeing it for the first time. Was the sun intended by our loving Creator to serve merely as a "heating stove" for this little Earth and its companion planets? Was it just a gigantic "hydrogen furnace" slowly consuming itself as it burns its supply of hydrogen fuel? Or could it be true that the SUN is a great and SHINING WORLD made brilliant not by flaming hydrogen gases, but rather by its own electromagnetic radiance?

My Venusian teacher had stated that the sun of our solar system is inhabited by wondrously glorified human beings, the "graduates" of this planetary system. He had mentioned something of the Solar Body that it was built of a more permanent electronic substance than our dense physical bodies are made of. And he had pointed out that the Solar Body was to be built by each of us gradually, over a period of several interplanetary incarnations. Also that it was a radiant LIGHT BODY, able to sustain the most intense solar light vibrations produced by the great SHINING WORLD (SUN)!

Life on Venus, then, was one mighty step nearer to our eventual HOME-the Sun-and it would seem that after we have perfected ourselves so as to take our place among the Sun People, another and greater goal would appear. Originally, all of humanity came from the Great Central Sun, or Supreme Sun. That is the greatest, most splendid world of all. It is located at the very center, or hub" of the universe (our Galaxy) and as it slowly revolves it causes every sun throughout the universe to revolve in harmony with it. As you will recall, you and I (and all beings) started our great Cosmic Journey from that center and were sent to the lesser sun of this solar system

THIS SIDE FOR STUDENT NOTES

for our "basic training" in matter. Thus, the sun that I watched drop gently behind the horizon, was in a sense more like my "home away from home". While beyond this sun, at an almost incredible distance, was my true home – the Supreme Sun. I could see then, that "the path of Return" – really meant returning in wisdom and glory to that most magnificent of all worlds at the hub of our Galaxy.

Once again I got into my car and drove up the winding Mountain Drive leading to that peaceful spot where Lon-Zara and I communicated telepathically with each other. The appointed time for the "mental rendezvous" was only minutes away. I was filled with eager anticipation at the thought of new wonders that my amazing friend would surely reveal to me within the next two hours. Indeed, my soul was already thrilled to its very depths by the marvels I had experienced from the first moment my Venusian master made known his presence to me via Telethot. Much greater things, however, were in store for me this evening, things that a few scant hours ago would have seemed above all reason.

I turned my car into the small clearing where I usually parked near the summit of the mountain, got out and sat down on the stone ledge overlooking the valley. Darkness was beginning to settle over the countryside. The sky sparkled with a few stars, and I could see the planet Venus most plainly of all. The night was warm, pleasant and friendly. I reached in my pocket and found the Telolith stone that had proven so helpful to me in my telepathic tests. Holding the Telolith in my right hand, my eyes again sought the planet Venus. It was at that moment that I saw a strange phenomenon.

THE STAR THAT WASN'T

From my position on the high ledge on the mountain, I could observe what seemed to be a star in the sky slightly below and to the left of Venus. Like any other star, this one appeared to hang motionless in the heavens, yet it differed from the others in one unusual respect. It blinked slowly, methodically and in brilliant changing hues of color; red, orange, green and blue. While I watched this strange "star" in fascination, the musical signal from Lon-Zara suddenly flooded into my awareness.

"Michael X" came that marvelous voice, "Greetings to you o from all of us who have watched your progress on Earth. At this moment I am closer to you than you realize, although I am certain you would have guessed the truth yourself had I not communicated with you now. That unusual star you are observing is not a star but a

THIS SIDE FOR STUDENT NOTES

Space Disc from Venus. I am aboard that Disc now and communing with you mentally from a position in space approximately 30 miles above the Earth."

"But," I said with the strangest sensation welling up in my throat, "only last evening you were on the planet Venus! That's twenty-six million miles away from our Earth. I don't see how..."

"How such a distance can be navigated in one day? This was accomplished, Beloved Brother, by traveling in our Space Disc at a velocity that would be considered impossible by most scientific minds on Earth. We flash through the vast gulf of interstellar space at a speed approaching that of light itself. To us, time and space have ceased to be factors of overly important significance, for at such velocities we have "collapsed" time and space to the point where they remain only pleasant and delightful "challenges" to us.

"The time has come," continued the Space Master, "for us to make ourselves known to more and more sincere individuals on your planet. We have found only a mere handful of Earthlings who are prepared to welcome us with open hearts and minds. But we are grateful for those few. You, Michael X, are one of several other chosen ones whom we shall visit and instruct before this night is over- Why are we here? To serve a very important purpose, a COSMIC PURPOSE which has to do with the spiritual aligning of Earthmen with the PLAN OF THE CREATOR. We come to assist those who are ready, to make the next higher step upward in soul-revolution. This is the reason for our visits to Earth, to save your world from the elements that would destroy it through the Forces of Negative and to bring certain individuals the PATTERN whereby a better world CAN and SHALL be built.

A CENTRAL GROUP OF ELDER BROTHERS HEADED BY JESUS

"The Earth is undergoing a Great Awakening," Lon-Zara said, "for the call has gone out from the higher realms for more enlightenment on planet Earth. The Overseers of this mighty movement include the Lords of Venus, Mercury and Vulcan, which are headed by our brother who is known to you as Jesus. All who hear the call and respond to it, are tested by us first. Those who wish to serve with us must meet one requirement...they must be selfless in service to the Wise Ones. This is possible only if one has love and compassion for the divine LIFE that dwells in humanity.

THIS SIDE FOR STUDENT NOTES

"Step back to the edge of the clearing, my Brother." the Adept suddenly commanded. "Our Space Disc is about to descend near you. Move back quickly!"

Obeying the command at once, I stepped back away from the central clearing as fast as I could. With unbelievable speed and absolute silence the "star" became an ever increasing body of whitish blue light as it flashed toward me. It grew larger by the second and glowed intermittently with several different colors. I could see it was circular in shape, with an outer section spinning rapidly. The light from the "saucer" or disc was intensely brilliant, but appeared to me to be more phosphorescent than fiery. In diameter, the disc must have been twenty-five feet across. For a moment it hovered over the center of the clearing, and then settled almost to the ground. There, a few feet above the earth, it hung motionless. A gentle sound was now audible. Like the quiet humming of bees. Then the disc floated to the ground, and all the bright glowing light disappeared.

In a state akin to shock, I watched a door in the side of the Space Disc open silently, in front of me. A man of tall and commanding stature stepped out of the amazing craft. He was clad in a one-piece uniform which appeared to have been made of some amazingly flexible, pressure-resistant material. On seeing me, the Spaceman lifted his right hand in a universal gesture of friendship, and moved in my direction.

"Greetings, dear friend," he said, and as he spoke the words X recognized instantly the mellow tones of Lon-Zara's voice. My heart leaped with such sudden joy that I was left almost breathless. As he drew nearer I could see his face for the first time...It was the face of an extraordinarily intelligent human being, radiating masculine strength and decisiveness, but also conveying an inner quality of peace and kindliness and a compassion I shall never forget. His forehead was high and full and he had an abundance of golden-bronze hair which was parted in the middle. The color of his skin was somewhat unusual. It was of a golden-tan radiant hue, denoting an individual in perfect health.

A HIGHLY EVOLVED HUMAN BEING FROM ANOTHER PLANET

The Venusian adept looked directly at me. He had very large, clear, blue eyes which shone like precious jewels, with a great depth in them and. I felt as if I were looking into a deep ocean and could see the whole universe. Divine strength, love, heavenly wisdom radiated from those wondrous eyes. His expression was beyond my dream. Who knows how many thousands of years I had waited for this moment? Yet it seemed

THIS SIDE FOR STUDENT NOTES

to me that I had felt this same dynamic presence even before our first telepathic contact.

"Yes, my dear friend," said the master teacher from Venus, answering my unspoken thought. "I have often been in your presence and stood by your side, although you did not see me. I have directed the flow of ideas which streamed into your brain while you elaborated them and put them down in writing in your special monographs. Moreover, this place has often been visited by you while your physical body was sleeping and you have conversed with me and with other Venusians. But when your soul-body returned to its house of flesh and blood, it could not impress the memory of those meetings upon your Conscious brain centers. Therefore you could remember none of your transcendental SPACE TRAVELS when you awoke.

"The memory of the animal form retains only the impressions made upon it by the avenues of the five physical senses; the memory of the SOUL awakens when we are in the spiritual state."

I told Lon-Zara that I considered this day the happiest one in my life, and only regretted that I was not yet ready to begin active life on his planet, Venus, as I felt that I was not yet worthy to remain in the society of beings so far exalted above my own state. There are many reasons why it is difficult for us to each know our own "rating" in spiritual evolution.

"It is true," Lon-Zara said, "that you are not yet ready to become an active citizen of Venus, for your special work on Earth is by no means completed. You shall, however, be permitted to look in on our planet by MENTAL TELEVISION and thereby gain firsthand knowledge of our advanced way of life* This power, and others that we shall give you, are spiritual in nature and must never be misused. Unless they are used to serve the GREAT PURPOSE, they could prove harmful to you and to the race. Remember always that SOUL POWER is a divine privilege, and while the Lords of Venus can bestow power upon Earthlings, that power can also be turned off at the discretion of the Wise Ones!"

As the Venusian said this, his mild and benevolent look seemed to penetrate my whole being and to read my innermost thoughts. Then he smiled, closing his eyes momentarily. To my amazement and delight, another human being stepped out of the Space Disc and came over to where we were talking. I could see by the light diffused through the open door of the Disc, that it was a woman of unusual beauty. She too, wore the same kind of uniform, indigo blue in color, with an iridescent quality in it.

THIS SIDE FOR STUDENT NOTES

Her movements were graceful, dignified and yet full of youthful energy as she approached.

Like Lon-Zara, the Space-woman's skin was sun-bronzed and healthy looking. She too was fair-haired with a full high forehead. Her eyes were a rich blue-violet color in which a few tiny flecks of gold seemed to sparkle. Her features were beautifully proportioned, and her entire figure rather tall and slim. Around her waist she wore a golden belt of most unusual design. Her feet were clad in shoes made of a soft, golden mesh material of extreme pliability.

"Greetings from us both, Michael X," she said sweetly, in bell-like tones. "I am Shelana of Venus. We love you and the people of Earth as we do our own glorious world, but we are saddened to behold the inharmony of your planet. It is for this reason that we come to visit you and any others of the Earth who will listen to our voice. We bring to you the superlative science of Life, Love and Light from Venus, which can create a Positive New Earth for you, just as it brought Peace, Love and Abundance to Venus. Our mission on Earth is to find souls who will assist us in teaching the "Science" to men, women, and children everywhere on your globe.

We are looking for those of you who will help fulfill that purpose. As you now know, we are not aliens but your own Elder Brothers and Sisters who have trod the same path you now tread. Higher evolution is your next step, and we are here to guide those of you who have prepared themselves through discipline and meditation. By using the THREE PRIMARY PRINCIPLES, Life, Love and Light harmoniously, you shall establish a Positive world!"

It was indeed inspiring to hear Shelana speak these words of encouragement, and I at once perceived that she was not only beautiful but highly intelligent as well.

"Many of us Earthlings have long desired such a Positive world," I admitted, "but so far we have not discovered the right formula. The destructive way comes easier to some of us and as a bitter result our Earth reaps fear, hatred, disease and war. Yet, I have always believed that a universal formula exists in the Cosmos whereby humanity here can live in mutual respect and harmony."

Shelana and Lon-Zara did not speak. They did not need to, for their thought suddenly transformed my whole being, filling me with a hitherto unknown feeling of joy, beauty and serenity. I knew then that such a formula does indeed exist and is in use now by all advanced planets. I felt that love, properly understood, was the great

THIS SIDE FOR STUDENT NOTES

key. And love, in its higher aspect, is not spoken. It comes like a wonderful comforter to serve the innermost needs of all living souls.

THE MYSTERIOUS VENUSIAN EMBLEM AND ITS GREAT SIGNIFICANCE

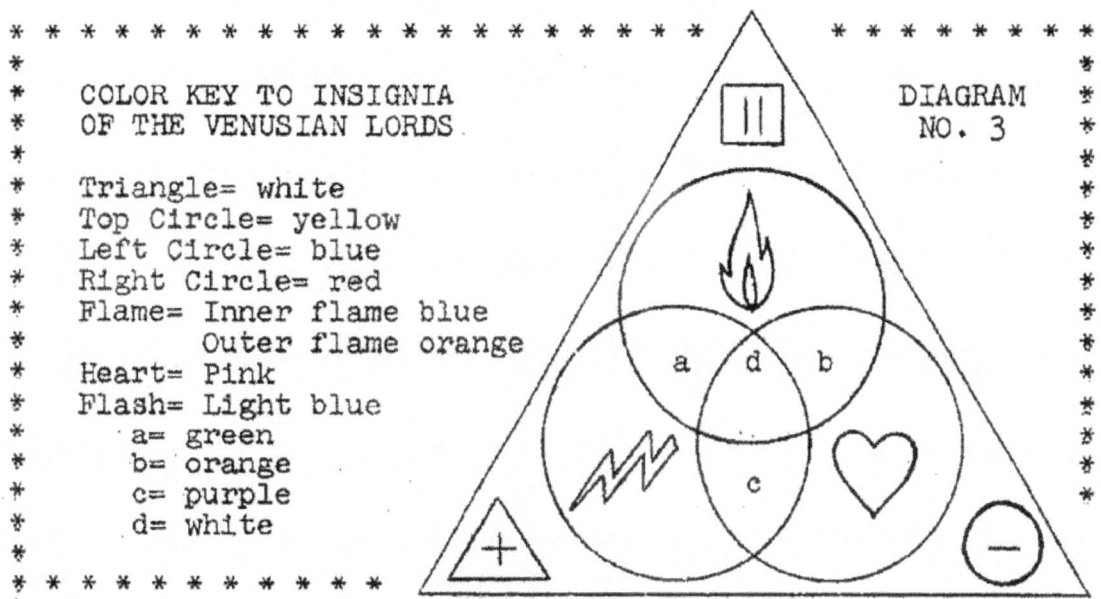

While I stood there, profoundly affected by the positive and uplifting soul vibrations of these two noble beings, I noticed with great interest the triangular-shaped emblem or insignia which each of my visitors wore on the breast of their uniform. The strange emblem glowed softly with a light of its own- It contained three intermeshed circles of blue, yellow and red colors. I could see several other symbols within the triangle.

"This insignia" said Lon-Zara, noting my interest, is worn by all Venusians who have, by study and application, qualified themselves to teach the SECRET SCIENCE. The symbols contained within this white triangle hold the answers to earth man's greatest problems, as you will come to understand later. At this moment, I call your attention to the three circles. Each circle is imbued with one of the THREE PRIMARY COLORS, blue, yellow and red. These colors signify the THREE PRIMARY PRINCIPLES by means of which the whole celestial universe is operated. Blue denotes the principle of LIEE or Universal God-Will. Red denotes the principle of LOVE or spiritual attraction. Yellow signifies the principle of LIGHT or Intelligent Reason.

THIS SIDE FOR STUDENT NOTES

Keep these three principles in mind as we progress, for they are the important keys to our superior powers.

"By interblending and balancing the three primary colors (or principles), FOUR other secondary colors result. As you notice, the four new colors are Green, Orange, Purple and Indigo. Each secondary color indicates a principle, thus Green signifies PEACE, Orange signifies JOY, Purple denotes POWER and Indigo symbolizes BEAUTY. By adding these four secondary principles to the first three primary ones, a total of SEVEN PRINCIPLES becomes manifest. Do you recall them?"

"Yes," I answered, for my memory seemed especially keen and retentive whenever Lon-Zara was instructing me, and I felt as if each word from him impressed a vivid image upon my mind, never to be forgotten. I repeated the Principles:

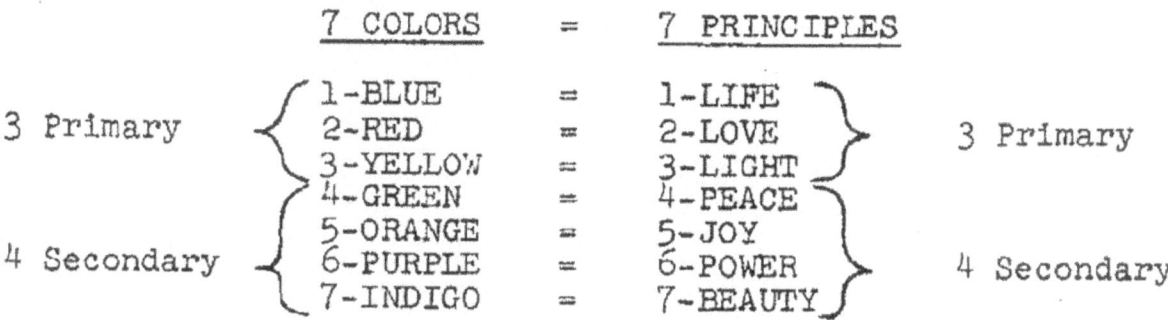

"Now," said Lon-Zara, "what happens when the element of black is added to each of the three Primary colors?"

"The three colors which originally are a cheerful and bright hue, would become dark, dull and drab." I replied.

Gazing directly into my eyes, the Venusian said, "You are right, and in precisely the same manner, if we add the element of darkness or NEGATIVITY to our three Primary Principles of LIFE, LOVE and LIGHT, the total effect is NEGATIVE. That is, the four secondary principles are obscured so that instead of manifesting all seven principles as FORCES OF POSITIVE, we would unhappily manifest their opposites, namely:

7 FORCES OF NEGATIVE

IGNORANCE

FEAR

THIS SIDE FOR STUDENT NOTES

HATRED

REVENGE

DISEASE

UGLINESS

DEATH

"However," Lon-Zara continued, "you must not make the mistake of presuming that, by practicing what your world calls "Positive Thinking", you will thereby eliminate automatically all the Forces of Negative. Positive thought is indeed useful and a step in the right direction. But as you well know, an individual can be exceedingly positive about the most negative, destructive and harmful things. An armed man can become a positive minded killer, a brilliant scientist can think so positively that he is able to assemble a guided missile which has as its sole purpose the mass destruction of many other human beings. Do you see now, how vitally important it is for humanity to find the TRUE FORMULA?"

"In this HYDROGEN BOMB age, with deadly intercontinental ballistic missiles, the need is more urgent than ever before in the history of the planet Earth," I remarked gravely.

"Happily for your Earth and all humanity, there is a way whereby the SEVEN CURSES (the Forces of Negative) can be eliminated from your planet," said Lon-Zara. "For it was by this same means that our own world, Venus, was transformed into a Positive Planet, radiating the FORCES OF POSITIVE. And what we accomplished, your people of Earth may also hope to achieve, with the assistance of our Venusian Lords."

HOW ALL MAN'S PROBLEMS MAY BE SOLVED

"Millions of years ago the greatest Thinkers of Venus discovered the true purpose and function of man's mind. They learned that all living beings, including man himself, are the manifested result of two primordial powers which are called Universal Will and Love, and which called the entire universe into existence. The two primal powers are in essence electrical (Will) and magnetic (Love) and as you have previously learned, are comprised of electrons and vitrons. These two forces may manifest in various ways

THIS SIDE FOR STUDENT NOTES

and on the seven different planes of existence, as mechanical force or as spiritual powers; but they are always the same divine primordial powers of Will (or Life) and Love (Mutual Attraction), acting through the instrumentality of the MIND of God the Father and His Hierarchy of Wise Ones, who direct the two great powers by INTELLIGENCE.

"Man's greatest mistake has been to imagine that he is an individual entity, having a will of his own, whose mode of action is different from the Universal Will. This serious mistake has been THE CAUSE of all individual, national and international problems of humanity on the Earth. The only solution lies in correcting the basic CAUSE. Earthlings will not be able to build a better world, a Positive Planet, until they understand this truth: Life or Will is a universal power. With it, all things live. Without it, all things die.

It causes the revolution of planets in space; it pervades and penetrates everything, and does not require your strengthening it, for it is already strong enough to accomplish everything possible. Your divine duty as a human being, is simply to RECOGNIZE the universal will and permit it to act and manifest freely through you. You may then experience the fullest extent of its strength...if you do not attempt to oppose it.

But if you ignore the universal will, and think that your personal human will is separate and superior to the great original power, what is the natural result? You merely divert an insignificant part of the life energy and oppose it to the original will-power of the universe; and as you are only an insignificant part of the latter, you will be overwhelmed by THE SEVEN CURSES and bring on your own destruction. Long ago we discovered that MAN'S function is to embody the third primary Principle which is LIGHT (or Intelligence).

When man uses his reason and intelligence he needs no "personal will" for he can then TUNE IN to the will of the universal Spirit, and utilize its unlimited power in a wise manner."

"Then," I said, ,fall of humanity's troubles come from its shortsightedness in ignoring the universal will, which I perceive to be the LAWS OF LIFE as found in all Nature. I can easily see how a human being, who tries to use his imagined "personal will" contrary to THE GREAT WILL, at once comes into conflict with infinitely greater power and is thus sooner or later BROKEN by the Law he, knowingly or unknowingly has opposed it."

THIS SIDE FOR STUDENT NOTES

LIGHT IS THE HIGHEST PRIMARY PRINCIPLE

"The TRUE FORMULA," replied the adept, is indicated by the position of the three circles shown in our insignia. You will note that the golden yellow circle is uppermost. There is a very good reason for this. It denotes the fact that the principle of LIGHT (Intelligence) is the highest principle in the universe; for by employing our Reason and Intelligence in harmony with the universal design (Peace and Good Will to all men) we may guide and conduct the already existing Life-Energy in Nature, and thereby cause it to accomplish marvelous things in perfect accordance with the laws of Nature. When a human being employs his Intelligence in tune with the God-Will (Good-Will to all beings) he or she is then overjoyed to find that SEVEN BLESSINGS begin to manifest in his or her life. Moreover, these blessings continue to increase the more the TRUE FORMULA is observed.

"The SEVEN BLESSINGS being the forces of Positive?" I asked, recalling again those seven wonderful principles.

"Truly," replied Lon-Zara, "real treasure is not outside of man, but within him. It consists of INTELLIGENCE, by which man may direct the force of his Spirit (Life) to create the GOOD he idealizes, and bring it forth in perfect order, harmony and peace. Harmony, you see, is LOVE. If the Creator of the Cosmos had used only blind force without love and intelligence, there never could have been an orderly creation.

"Yes," added Shelana, "Love is, we might say, cohesion, or a universal force that holds things together, keeping all things in right relationship to their source. What is the secret of achieving a "Love Consciousness"? It is simply to work in harmony with your source-Divine Spirit. Live, move and act in conscious awareness of LIFE, LOVE and LIGHT, knowing that by doing so you are keeping your life in divine and perfect order. These three primary principles are working in and through all living beings. This makes all life ONE. See the ONENESS, the unity of life and you can no longer think of yourself as separated from the one UNIVERSAL SOURCE. Of ourselves we can do nothing. It is the living Spirit that quickens, reanimates our thoughts and our bodies. Then we are able to express creative power and thereby perfect ourselves and our physical environment."

As I listened enraptured to these golden words of wisdom from my two wonderful Space friends, I felt this sense of oneness and it was indeed a profound experience. In one glorious moment I embraced THE ALL and enfolded that One Life with the light and love of my own soul and spirit. Suddenly I could see that the Science

THIS SIDE FOR STUDENT NOTES

of the Venusians was "secret" only to those who did not know and feel the unity of all LIFE. Surely the Space People could find many others on Earth who understood love's power. Those Earthlings could assist....

"Only a FEW are chosen," said Lon-Zara reading my mind. "Among the billions of Earthlings, simply because the majority are not physically, mentally, and most important of all, SPITUALLY EXPRESSING the higher vibrations of love. We can only assist those who are ready to receive our influence.

"We can only approach those who spiritually approach our own sphere. Love causes mutual attraction; evil repulses. The pure will be attracted to the pure, the evil ones to that which is impure. To give presupposes the capacity to receive on the part of him who is to receive. The SUNLIGHT is open to all, but not all are able to see it. The eternal fountain of COSMIC TRUTH is inexhaustible and universal; but those who open their hearts to the REALITY of our presence are few. We come in peace, seeking our own...those who recognize us and can see as we do the great need for WORLD ENLIGHTENMENT.

"Those who wish to contact us," said the Venusian, "may prove their sincerity of purpose by concentrating their full attention upon our VENUSIAN INSIGNIA, for FIVE or more minutes daily. The insignia should first be colored with all the correct colors. While concentrating, the student should meditate deeply upon the profound significance of the three primary principles, LIFE, LOVE & LIGHT; and their four secondary's, PEACE, JOY, POWER & BEAUTY. At the conclusion of each concentration period, the student should mentally invoke their own true Cosmic Teacher from Venus. This practice will assist in putting the individual in rapport with us and, at the same time, will expand his spiritual awareness. We will then lead him gradually—by silent means—first to one little thing, then to another, along the Path of Return, until at last he is evolved to that point where one of us will become his personal Teacher. He will then be guided to a visible contact such as you have experienced. Mysteries will be made plain to him at that time, which would be dangerous to seek without the aid of one of the Elder Brothers.

THIS SIDE FOR STUDENT NOTES

SPECIAL QUESTIONS: The theme of this third lesson suggests the following important questions:

1. What does the Path of Return really mean?

2. Do you believe that a "universal formula" exists whereby human beings everywhere can live in peace and harmony?

3. Name the three primary principles and their colors.

4. Name the four secondary principles and the colors.

5. What has been the greatest mistake of Earth man?

THIS SIDE FOR STUDENT NOTES

YOUR GRADUATION FROM EARTH

Lesson 4

WHILE Lon-Zara was instructing me as to the method by which sincere individuals on Earth may invoke the aid of the Space People, and come into attunement with one or more of the Cosmic Teachers on Venus, Shelana had quietly walked back to the Space Disc at the center of the clearing. She entered the craft and after a few moments reappeared at the door. In her right hand she carried a small tray. The tray held three large golden chalices, each one filled with a creamy, sparkling liquid. Walking over to where Lon-Zara and I stood, Shelana smiled, saying:

"My Brothers, forgive my momentary absence. I have prepared a delicious tropical elixir for each of us. It is a custom of our people to partake often of liquid refreshment."

The suggestion was most welcome, for in my excitement over tonight's contact with these two wonderful beings, I had forgotten completely about any need for nourishment. And, as I had by-passed my usual supper, I looked forward happily to the refreshing elixir Shelana had prepared for us. If this elixir was made from foods grown on the planet Venus, it would no doubt possess a flavor quality unknown to Earthlings.

Shelana served to each of us a golden chalice, full to the brim of the creamy liquid. Lon-Zara proposed a toast:

"Let us drink to LIFE, LOVE and LIGHT on Earth!"

We did so, and its wonderful effect made me gasp with a pleasant surprise. Not only was the taste of the beverage exquisitely delicious, as though it had been concocted from some truly ambrosial tropical fruit, but the electrically vivifying action

THIS SIDE FOR STUDENT NOTES

of the Elixir was immediate and positive. Whereas I had felt somewhat weak and lacking in energy, I now felt entirely refreshed and amazingly strengthened.

THE MAGIC OF VITALITY ELIXIRS

"That which you drank," Lon-Zara explained, "is but one of many such Vitality Elixirs we enjoy regularly every day on Venus. We prepare these unusual beverages from various tropical and sub-tropical fruits which abound in positive electric qualities as well as being delightfully delicious to the taste. By drinking these special food elixirs consistently, the men and women of Venus realize superior health and preserve their youthful looks for several centuries. Of course we have other means whereby we are able to live long enough in one particular body to attain a high state of Conscious evolvement in. mind and body. If Earth man but knew it, this also is his goal, for by rightly directing the divine energies of LIFE and LOVE he would thereby build for himself and all mankind, a state of HEAVEN and HARMONY on Earth as well as in the hereafter. A time is coming when such a harmonious condition shall exist on your planet, and it will be manifested by intelligent men and women who realize that all three of these PRIMARY POWERS, Life, Love and Divine Wisdom (Light) act from within each individual. Self-knowledge is the basic need of your people. When you know that the "Divine Trinity Principles" are operative within every person, all that is then required is a program of WORLD ENLIGHTENMENT to put those principles into ACTIVE USE."

THE COMING MILLENIUM

"Life, Love and Light," I said, "are the true forces, then, that shall usher in another Golden Age on Earth. For I see now that a prophesied thousand years of peace and good-will on. Earth* is but the secondary effect of those three primary CAUSES."

"True," replied Lon-Zara, "your long-awaited Millennium is nearer than you realize. Still, we have not the time to wait for it. Each individual on Earth has a most important task to perform right now. Let each one attempt to restore harmony in his own mind, body and soul by RECOGNIZING the universal nature of LIFE, LOVE and LIGHT. The next step is to actually live according to these three principles, to the utmost of your understanding. This will automatically bring you into "tune" or harmony with ALL OF NATURE'S LAWS since they are but secondary manifestations

THIS SIDE FOR STUDENT NOTES

of the three primary principles. This may be somewhat strange and difficult to do at first, but will become easier and more satisfying as you persist in living from the 'Soul Center'. Then harmony of your planet as a whole will be restored and the Earth will come into its own era of Peace, Power and Plenty!"

GRADUATING FROM THIS EARTHLIFE

"Am I correct in thinking that each of the seven sacred planets—of which Earth is one—has its own individual Heavenworlds where the souls on that planet go to rest after the physical body dies?" I asked.

"We have found it to be so," the master answered, "for it Is part of the COSMIC PLAN that each soul must ascend to the kingdom of the SUN (THE GREAT SHINING WORLD) by mastering the negative conditions of each physical planet. This is called the overcoming of matter by the spirit. It is in no way a violent process, but rather a series of gradual steps by which man starts his climb (great Cosmic Journey) at the bottom rung of the Ladder (planetary system) and progresses slowly from planet to planet until he reaches the top of the ladder. Hermes Mercurlus Trismegistus, one of the twelve great Teachers of Earth's humanity, taught this same truth when he said: 'To know Divine thought, o souls, you must descend and painfully ascend the paths of the SEVEN PLANETS and of their SEVEN HEAVENS.'

"Then," I said, "what the average person considers to be his ultimate destination, i.e. Heaven, is not the real goal at all, for you say there is a 'heaven1 around each of the planets, making a total of SEVEN HEAVENS. Yet each of these is only a revisiting place' en route to the SUN?"

"Yes. Each planet is surrounded by its own astral or etheric worlds; the highest of which is called a heaven. When a human being on any planet dies, the soul leaves the physical body, and in its astral body enters first into the lower astral frequencies of ATMOSPHEREA. Most usually at death the individual goes into a period of 'Soul-Sleep' or unconsciousness (this period varies with different souls) during which period he dwells for a time in his astral body.

As this fades, he lives only in the point form, or 'Divine Atom'. This Divine Atom then slowly gravitates into higher regions of the etheric world until it attains the more blissful, heavenly regions of ETHERIA.

THIS SIDE FOR STUDENT NOTES

"During its sojourn or 'sleep' in the lower astral frequencies next to the planet, the soul gradually awakens from its deep dreamless sleep and as it rises higher and higher in the etheric regions, begins to dream and create vivid mental pictures of the things and sensations it most loved and desired while on the material plane of planetary life. As the dream takes on more and more sense of urgency to manifest, a universal law of Rebirth becomes automatically operative and the individual soul is drawn magnetically (by thought and desire) back to the material world and 'wakes up' in a new physical body. With some good souls there is an urgency to 'come back and try again' to pass certain 'tests' in the planet's objective life-plane. Bear in mind, though, that there has been, in this rebirth, no actual PROGRESSION to a new and more advanced planet. This does not take place until the individual has been reborn so many times on a particular planet that he or she has consciously developed a greater knowledge of LIFE, LOVE and LIGHT. From this knowledge WISDOM is born. Wisdom is derived from experience of the soul in the material state. And the purpose of wisdom is to enable man to release himself from physical cravings, appetites and sensations which 'magnetize' him or her to one physical world.

"The law of Rebirth works on a magnetic principle. On your planet Earth, for instance, a soul who has just newly arrived must begin its Earthlife in one to twelve months. These worlds are composed of finer grades or 'densities' of matter and are invisible to ordinary physical sight. Each month of the Earth year is but one small division of the GREAT ZODIACAL CIRCLE, yet each month bestows upon the soul a different planetary influence than any of the other months. In order for a soul to gain all the qualities of the 12 Zodiacal periods and thereby acquire COMPLETE experience from the planet Earth, it rotates through each of the Zodiacal Signs by a series of successive rebirths. Each new rebirth on the Earth adds to the completeness of the soul's experience.

THE WAY OF REBIRTH

"By the time a soul has completed twelve REBIRTH Zodiacal Rounds (a total of 144 Earth lives) it should – if it has been diligent – have overcome its animal nature and mastered its physical appetites. If so, the gravitational pull of the planet Earth can no longer hold it and draw it back to Earth for more embodiments. The soul has become more POSITIVE and hence is drawn magnetically toward the next higher advanced planet. This is known as THE GREAT DAY of the souls graduation1 from a less evolved world to a more spiritual and advanced planet."

THIS SIDE FOR STUDENT NOTES

"What happens," I inquired, "if a soul refuses to apply itself and fails to gain enough WISDOM to enable it to master its negative nature and overcome the pull of gravity?"

"Several undesirable things may happen." the master replied, "For one, the soul will remain Earthbound and be drawn back into another cycle of TWELVE earth lives in order to make up for what it missed learning in the previous cycle. It cannot be permitted to 'graduate' until it has learned through its experiences to RECOGNIZE the primary principles of LIFE, LOVE and LIGHT. Each successive cycle of twelve rotations is much harder than the first, for only by severe trials and tests does such a soul begin to manifest WISDOM.

PLANETARY LAGGARDS

"Perhaps the most unpleasant result of not keeping up with your fellow Classmen in the planetary school of life, is that the 'student' who falls to graduate with the others will eventually find himself in the company of much younger souls from less advanced planets such as Mars. Those younger souls find it quite difficult to 'understand' the older soul. And so it is always better not to become a 'planetary laggard', for those who do not keep pace with their particular Life Wave or group, are bound to find their planetary experiences more uncomfortable. The solution to this problem is not complicated, but it does require a greater exertion of effort on the part of the ones who are 'backward' in their planetary progress. If they are sincere in desiring to catch up with their original group, they should seek to obtain as much WISDOM as possible from each experience in their daily life. Instead of looking at outer effects only, they should make it a special point to look beneath the surface of things, into the inner CAUSES of the effects they see. They roust learn to discover these causes for themselves, and not rely on others to do the mental work for them. As an example: if an individual becomes ill, he should first search his own past actions to discover the true cause of his illness. For unless he recognizes his own mistakes by using his own intelligence, he can have no permanent health.

"Without wisdom one cannot advance to the next higher planet, and wisdom comes through SELF-KNOWLEDGE and a deeper understanding of the natural laws of life. To make sure of your graduation, therefore, double and redouble your efforts to KNOW THYSELF, for if you do this, you will begin to know how the Microcosm (the Small Universe) functions. Then, by analogy, you will at once begin to comprehend

THIS SIDE FOR STUDENT NOTES

how the Macrocosm (the Great Universe) is designed, for truly 'as it is below, so it is above' as it is in the lesser, so it is in the larger LIFE, LOVE and LIGHT govern all things.

PHYSICAL DEATH IS NOT INEVITABLE

"I have mentioned previously that it is entirely possible to forestall death of your physical body for indefinite lengths of time, if certain natural law's and practices are observed. On Venus, the men and women do not age as rapidly as do your people of Earth. Evergreen youthfulness is the rule rather than the exception on Venus. To live for 500 to 1000 years in one physical body is not uncommon for our people. Does this fact startle you? It need not, for remember that the average Venusian is near the level of Adeptship, and if you will recall some of Earth's Adepts have been able to prolong the appearance of youthful vigor for several centuries."

"Master," I exclaimed, "How is this great extension of physical life in the same bodily form possible? As you well know, the people of Earth consider it a marvelous thing if they succeed in reaching the old age of 100 years. Despite the efforts of our men of science, the average person finds it exceedingly difficult to prolong his life. I have noticed that in most cases, the human body starts to 'break down' at about age 40, and becomes less and less efficient from then on. So-called old age (65 yrs and over) is usually associated with weakness, disease and untimely death, just at the time when the individual is beginning to gain some real wisdom and could thus be of most value and usefulness to the world."

"Neither a plant nor an animal, nor a human being can be expected to live and grow healthfully unless it receives the food and the stimulus it requires," replied Lon-Zara.

But unfortunately the average Earthling has never taken time to think out the question of VITAL NUTRITION to its logical conclusion. So instead of consulting Mother Nature to find out what classes of natural food she intended him to partake of for his health and longevity, Earth man has come to the conclusion that he is OMNIVOROUS and hence may eat anything that grows, swims, walks or runs, so long as it is not another human being. The result of this omnivorous attitude regarding food has caused man to eat abundantly of animal flesh, animal by-products and the various cereal grains which were never designed for man's sustenance. In order to make these foods palatable enough to eat, it was necessary to cook them by fire and then add salt

THIS SIDE FOR STUDENT NOTES

and spices to them for flavor. By submitting nearly all of his food to fire, man destroyed the ELECTRIC principle in those foods. Also, the fire destroyed the living enzymes which aid in digesting the food. Man was thereby forced to supply living enzymes from his own body.

"Our Venusian scientists discovered long ago that the KEY to youthful longevity is VITO-ELECTRICITY and LIVING ENZYMES. Where are these marvelous factors to be obtained? Only from vital, living plants, such as tender, succulent vegetables, luscious fruits, melons and berries, and the oleaginous seeds and nuts of various kinds. When these foods are eaten in their natural state just as they come from Nature, they are rich in SOLAR ENERGY which is able to animate all the atomic cells of your human body, stimulating it naturally with electric essence from the sun's rays. In addition to this, such foods provide a plentiful supply of living enzymes which assist digestion. Moreover, these foods are most delicious when uncooked. Thus they require no seasoning by salt, pepper and spices which irritate the body but add nothing to it in the way of ELECTRICAL VITALITY.

"In order to live long and healthfully, Earthlings need only follow the guiding hand of Nature, and eat food as far as possible in its natural state and uncooked. To submit any food to the action of fire at once injures the positive principle in that food, and destroys its enzymes. The extent may be little or great, but the effect is bound to show up sooner or later in life as DESTRUCTIVE to the body. When a body is deprived of enzymes through a steady diet of cooked food, year in and year out, it must work extra hard in order to produce enough enzymes to digest that food. By so doing it overworks the glands, weakens them and ages the body in a futile attempt to supply ENZYMIC ELEMENTS. In time, therefore, the tired cells become clogged with their wastes and have not enough power, to throw off the poisons. Premature old age, disease and death are the sad effects of eating wrong foods (which require cooking) instead of enjoying right foods which can be eaten as Nature prepared them. It is all so wonderfully simple when man observes Nature's Plan which of course follows the UNIVERSAL WILL of the Creator.

"However, the moment that man voluntarily steps off Nature's Path and eats wrong foods, the problem of health becomes increasingly complex, confusing and bewildering. It is for this very reason that those Earthlings who would prepare their physical bodies for the phenomenal changes that are taking place and shall take place as we enter the NEW AGE, should not permit themselves to be misled any further by man's mere whims and fancies, which appeal to unnatural cultivated appetites; but

THIS SIDE FOR STUDENT NOTES

should return to the sane simplicity of THE COSMIC PLAN. With the right food one can purify and regenerate the physical body, and make it a fit vehicle for New Age forces from the higher realms of light.

"This return to a simple, wholesome diet of natural foods consisting of the fruits of the earth, oleaginous seeds and nuts (or raw nut butters), nut milks, sprouted seeds and tender vegetables, must not be adopted suddenly. Rather it should be gradually replacing the old diet over a period of months until the body has lost all desire for the false foods of the fo1d Man' and developed a natural, normal preference for the VITAL, ELECTRIC, ENZYMIC foods of the 'NEW AGE MAN & WOMAN'. Remember, if you are not yet on the VITAL DIET; do not attempt to force your body to change overnight. Give it sufficient time to get accustomed to the new program by gradually increasing the amounts of natural foods consumed, and decreasing the amounts of unnatural foods.

THE HIDDEN WAY OF "COMMUNION"

"I have spoken to you about the great importance of building your SOLAR BODY or body of Light, in order that you may advance beyond the Earth, beyond Venus, even beyond Vulcan to the Sun itself. I wish now to explain that right food is a positive aid in raising the body's vibrations, for it permits SOLAR energies to travel more freely through your body. Thus your body will develop more light; for vibration traveling through matter creates light. It is for this reason that the roasters, including your great Teacher, Jesus, were careful to partake only of natural, vitalizing foods at all times. In addition to that, they fasted frequently to rid their bodies of cell wastes which would interfere with the inflow of SOLAR FORCE.

"When the Solar Force enters abundantly into the body of a master or adept who is prepared to receive it, and energizes the spiritual organs (Pineal and Pituitary glands), such a master may consciously 'step-up' the vibrational frequency of those organs to such a degree that he is able to communicate with higher beings of inconceivable grandeur and beauty. These mighty beings not only advise, but cooperate with the master so that he is enabled to carry out special missions in line with the GREAT COSMIC PLAN. It is by developing the SOLAR BODY and controlling the influx of Solar Force into the higher brain centers, that the adepts on Venus (as well as on the Earth) are able to 'tune-in' telepathically to the mental wave-lengths of

THIS SIDE FOR STUDENT NOTES

the highest beings in the universe, and receive the vibrations and instructions desired for higher service to the Cosmos.

"This Solar Force creates an actual 'arc of energy' within the brain of the adept, as the solar current flows through the spiritual centers in the head. By consciously stepping-up the voltage of this energy, an adept can cause his third density body (physical) to vibrate at the fourth density frequency (etheric) at will. His body thus becomes filled with electrical radiance which grows increasingly more brilliant until the vibratory rate corresponds to that of the fourth density. His physical body is then completely invisible to ordinary sight,

"Solar Force also serves to purify and vitalize the physical body to such a pronounced degree that it destroys all disease and if wisely directed, can overcome the 'Grim Reaper' – Death itself! Does not your Christian Bible prophesy that Man shall conquer his 'last great enemy' Death?

ENOCH, ELIJAH AND JESUS

"Thus by observing physical, mental and spiritual laws as they exist truly in Nature, your own great Teachers, Enoch, Elijah and the Master Jesus overcame death and 'by-passed' the Law of Rebirth by learning to govern the Solar Force so that by means of it they could raise their vibrations and perfect an imperishable SOLAR BODY. After their work on Earth was completed, these three Teachers were transported in space vehicles to Venus, where they convened with 'The Ancient of Days', Sanat Kumara, as to the results accomplished and the next phase of their Great Cosmic Work in helping Planet Earth.

"It is the chosen duty of advanced Venusians to assist you, our brothers and sisters, for we have walked the same paths you are now treading. We are like you, Sons and Daughters of THE GREAT LIGHT, the only difference being that we have had more time in which to perfect ourselves and ascend to the next step beyond your present level. You may consider us your Elder Brothers, ready, willing and able to serve you. Our dedicated task is the raising of the Earthlings, so that ever-increasing LIFE, LOVE and LIGHT shall radiate over your planet in the wonderful Age of Aquarius. According to the universal law of Mutual Attraction, those of you who are now developing a higher awareness of the beauty, goodness and oneness of all life will be attracted to Venus for your next incarnation. It is for this reason that on Venus you will find the highest type of teachers, philosophers, artists, poets and creative thinkers

THIS SIDE FOR STUDENT NOTES

of every class. Those Earthlings whose minds and hearts have not yet been opened to the great power of ENLIGHTENED LOVE, will not 'graduate' at their next incarnation, but will reincarnate again on the Earth. This will continue until they have attained a consciousness that is in more perfect harmony with the selfless and altruistic souls on the next higher planet."

As Lon-Zara finished this thought, a violet light began to blink on and off rapidly, above the door of the Space Disc.

"That is the signal," explained the Venusian, "for me and Shelana to return to the Great Transport Spaceship which is waiting for us at a stationary position 200 miles above the Earth. The small flying Saucer you see before you now is one of many 'Scout Discs' carried by the larger craft. We utilize these smaller discs for purposes of observing the Earth more closely and for making personal contacts with our friends here.

"Our Transport Spaceship will remain in its present position for three more days, during which time we shall commune with you telepathically each evening. It will not be necessary for you. to come to this mountainside as previously. The privacy of your own room in the city will be sufficient. However, you may continue to use a Telolith gem as before, to increase your powers of psychic attunement with us. Our next contact then will be by Telethot tomorrow evening at the usual hour. I shall at that time disclose to you some fascinating details regarding our way of life on Venus, and the wonderful souls who now dwell there."

Lon-Zara and Shelana smiled...beautiful, radiant, soul-warming smiles. I responded with a sincere smile and my most grateful thanks for the divine privileges they had bestowed upon me this night. My heart was too full to say more.

"Keep faith with us, Beloved Friend," said Lon-Zara, "and with the Divine Plan of the Cosmos, and your reward shall exceed your fondest hopes!"

With this, my two marvelous visitors turned quickly, and in a few graceful strides had reached the Flying Saucer and entered it. The door closed silently behind them. Then, as I watched in amazement, the circular craft suddenly glowed with brilliant, greenish light. This turned into intense golden orange, and all at once the ship was off the ground.

THIS SIDE FOR STUDENT NOTES

In seconds it climbed straight up for a distance of 300 feet, then changed direction and moved with unbelievable speed at an upward angle. The gold-orange color of the ship turned to blue-white and suddenly I could see it no longer.

SPECIAL QUESTIONS

The theme of this Fourth Lesson suggests the following five important Questions:

1. How may each individual on Earth restore harmony in his own body, mind and soul?

2. What is the number of "Heavens" each soul shall experience en-route to the Kingdom of the Sun?

3. State the number of Zodiacal Rounds of Rebirths usually required for complete experience on Earth. How many earth lives does this represent?

4. To make sure of your Graduation to Venus, what must you do right now in your present Earth-life?

5. What kind of individuals gravitate to Venus?

THIS SIDE FOR STUDENT NOTES

YOUR MAGIC LIFE ON VENUS
Lesson 5

THE next morning proved to be a busy one, as there were numerous routine duties to take care of in the office. I attended to these matters as carefully as I was able to, considering that my previous night's experiences had made a profound impression upon my mind. In memory I kept seeing the beautiful, radiant face of Shelana and the dynamic, compassionate expression of Lon-Zara. Golden memories these, and to think that these wonderful space-beings had not only given me "CSC" (Outer Space Communication), but had also honored me with a personal visitation by "flying saucer", was more than I could fully comprehend. Yet the inner assurance that I now felt was definite and positive. The space-beings did exist. They were real. This I knew now beyond the shadow of a doubt.

Moreover, there was real purpose in their being. Lon- Zara had made plain many secrets of Life which had been only deep mysteries to me before. He had taught me about the laws of planetary progression, rebirth, vital diet and of the great importance of building a Solar Body. I could see now that all this was in perfect alignment with the GREAT COSMIC PLAN of the Supreme Being. The wise ones from Venus were serving that Plan...not by violent force, but by a restraining influence of loving-kindness. Not by taking away from us what we have already acquired, but by adding to destructive Earthlings the necessary factors to make us constructive - HARMONIOUS.

Humanity on Earth has reached the decisive mid-point in planetary progression; but is greatly behind where it should be in SPIRITUALITY. To remedy this, the Venusians, our own elder "Space Brothers" are teaching us by personal example, how we too may assist in furthering THE GREAT PLAN.

THIS SIDE FOR STUDENT NOTES

I resolved to start at once applying what I had already been taught regarding the "Secret-Science", which, as you know, is based on living from one's inner "Soul Center" rather than from mere outer appearances. The first step, according to Lon-Zara, was to RECOGNIZE the universal nature of LIFE, LOVE and LIGHT. Very well...from now on I would consciously be more highly aware that I dwell in a LIVING universe, with every entity (mineral, plant, animal and human) partaking of ONE great Life. Also, every entity is evolving into a state of self-consciousness wherein it at last recognizes its own divinity. LIFE is the great Positive (+). It is the "Universal Father" of all creation.

Next I considered the second principle, LOVE. Looking about me I saw evidences everywhere of the presence of love. Not simply human affection, hut rhythm and harmony which keeps things, people and thoughts in ORDER instead of chaos and con-fusion. I looked at my own office desk. It was cluttered with papers that should have been filed neatly away. Only by putting those papers in order would I be able to create and build anything constructive from them. Love was not only a visionary thing; it was intensely PRACTICAL as well. It is by our use of Love that we are able to bring order and harmony into our daily lives, and thus brings forth some useful and constructive result. In this manner we are able to use the tools and talents we possess, to CREATE things of beauty and value for the human race.

NON-DESTRUCTIVE ACTIVITY IS THE KEYNOTE OF LOVE

Without sufficient Love-orderly activity-we always lack CONSTRUCTIVE power. The solution is to become more consciously aware of this principle of order, right relationship, neatness in every one of our daily actions. You have heard that "Love is the fulfilling of the Law", and truly it is. For the Law is LIFE. It is to "have LIFE and have it more abundantly" as the Master Jesus proclaimed. And by the practical means of useful, CREATIVE activity, you and I and all mankind produce the most desirable conditions for the manifestation of still GREATER LIFE. In all our activities there is no need to use brute force. Love never seeks to take things apart, only to harmonize. Add to Instead of take away. That is the secret. Intelligence guides Love. By being more ORDERLY we become more constructive and CREATIVE and success soon becomes automatic.

As I went about my daily routine, I began to recognize Love as being the "Universal Mother", the force that protects all Life by keeping it "well ordered and

THIS SIDE FOR STUDENT NOTES

secure". The same law applies to man as it does to great universes. Love is signified by the minus sign (-) to denote that it serves the Universal Will by cooperating with it non-destructively.

In addition to this practice of giving more conscious attention to the existence of the trinity principles, I also determined to make sure that my daily diet consisted of 100# vital foods. These were to be in the natural state, uncooked and unprocessed by man. In line with Lon-Zara's suggestions, I laid out for myself a real, "New Age Diet" and began to get accustomed to it by easy stages. Breakfast consisted of delicious fresh fruit with almond nut-milk; Lunch included a salad made of tender green leafy vegetables, sprouted alfalfa seeds, grated carrots, sliced cucumber and homemade salad dressing. Untoasted wheat germ was sprinkled liberally over this salad, and the result was a most delectable dish. Supper comprised a different kind of fruit with more of the nut-milk. This in brief, was my basic program. I began to prefer it to my "old" ways of living and eating.

During the day, I tried to imagine how it would be to live on a planet where negative conditions no longer exist to "hamper human progress". Venus must surely be such a planet. Somehow, the great and wise Lords of Venus had discovered the secret of developing a truly constructive, creative and Godlike race of beings. What that secret might be I could not guess. No doubt it was based on the practical knowledge and application of the "Trinity Principles", Life, Love and Light. Then too, Venus is Earth's elder Sister. Inhabitants on Venus have had millions of years more time than we, in which to develop and practice their Secret-Science.

EARTH IS A HARD SCHOOL

I thought of the many "negative ordeals" we Earthlings go through while we are here on this planet. The list is long and impressive. But it all adds up to a great big negative. To mention only a few of Earth's extremely undesirable conditions, consider: DISEASE (a vast host of ills which cut man down In his very prime), FACTORY STRIKES, (people out of work for weeks at a time) LAYOFFS, (good workers fired because of a decline in business, or because the company thinks a younger man or woman can do the Job better) MONEY INFLATION (in which the purchasing power of the dollar becomes less and less) TAXES, NATIONAL DEPRESSIONS (the fact that money is hoardable and earns interest for you if you keep it out of circulation

THIS SIDE FOR STUDENT NOTES

depresses the economy of the nation and creates debt. Idle money creates poverty, envy, hatred and war)...a host of ills.

Then there is the problem of SMOG in cities like Los Angeles, San Francisco and others. This is a negative condition that as yet has not been solved by our scientists. Yet SMOG has been proved a serious factor in undermining the health of men, women and children. Those whose livelihood depends upon working in such cities have to remain in them and "put up with the breathing of polluted air".

There is hope however. The Venusians have said that there will be a time in the near future when American leaders will pass laws curtailing the burning of coal and other pollutants. The air will improve and the water will run clean in places where it was once devoid of life. Unfortunately, there will be a President, and an entire political party, that will be in league with the DARK FORCES. Everything that previous administrations had done to benefit humanity: universal medical care, education, minority rights, stopping pollution and social injustice, the dark-forces President will rescind and destroy with obvious glee. His soul is blackened with physical and monetary lust, as well as a desire for ultimate control and POWER. He will divide the country like no President has ever done before...yet his followers will herald him as a savior who is bringing the United States back into renown and world power.

This time could be the breaking point for our country. We can avoid this if we push aside our petty hatreds, greed and jealousies and work together, not only as a country, but as members of the human family. The dark-forces that strive to undermine planet earth will use HATRED of those who are different: white against black...misogyny, homosexuals, etc., much like what took place in Germany in the 1930s. The Venusians have said that this point in our history doesn't have to occur, but if it does, it will herald an even more disastrous future for our planet.

The WEATHER DISASTERS take their toll of human lives as Earthman has no real control over the weather and can only try to protect himself against the freezing cold of blizzards, the lashing fury of hurricanes, tornadoes and floods which manifest on earth many times every year. CRIME also, in a multitude of forms takes its heavy toll not only of human lives but also of man's peace of mind and soul, hourly on the globe.

FOOD PROCESSING is another negative factor in Earth-life. God's naturally vital, nutritious foods of the Earth are taken by man and subjected to ungodly

THIS SIDE FOR STUDENT NOTES

processes such as pickling roasting, toasting, boiling, freezing, dehydrating, pasteurizing, frying and so forth until modem man is hard put to it to find food that still has LIFE left in it. Happily, the "Organic Movement" is growing in popularity in the United States and this is a big help. It believes that food should be grown in rich, organic soil and that the use of chemical fertilizers and poisonous sprays should not be used. The ever-present THREAT OF WAR is with us Earthlings, to increase our miseries. People of America live in fear of being blown to bits by atomic, hydrogen bombs from Russia. As for the people of Russia, they live in fear of being disintegrated by hydrogen bombs shot from America. Both sides are working overtime to make more bombs and guided missiles "just in case" a push-button war should rear its ugly head.

It would be easy to list many more conditions on Earth that humanity finds exceedingly unpleasant, if not entirely "Hellish". However, there's no need to go into grim details. You know them as well or possibly better than I do. The only conclusion is, our Earth IS a hard school. And for Just this very reason, those of us who graduate from Earth's "School of Hard Knocks" will be more spiritually powerful than those under favorable conditions on other planets who haven't yet learned how to MASTER all that is negative.

After I'd finished my day's work, I enjoyed a simple, wholesome and delightful supper at home, and then began my usual preparations for Telethot communication with Lon-Zara. I looked forward eagerly to hearing about the Venusians mode of life, and how it compared with our own life on the Earth. At 6:30 P.M. I made mental contact.

"Greetings, my Brother," spoke the velvet smooth voice of my Venusian Teacher, "I can see, by reading the electronic thought pattern of your subconscious mind that you have been thinking deeply today on the power and meaning of the THREE Principles. We are glad that you are beginning to apply the instructions given you, for it is by application of truths that you shall gain mastery of all that is undesirable."

"Yes, Lon-Zara," I replied, "your personal visitation last evening has expanded ray mind and soul to a deeper understanding of all that you have told me. I am open to whatever you may wish to teach me, for I know that not only myself but all humanity on Earth are in great need of your Cosmic Wisdom. It is my innermost conviction that the Secret-Science of Venus can and shall assist in bringing the Positive conditions into being on this Earth. We are tired of living with FEAR!"

THIS SIDE FOR STUDENT NOTES

"Fear is one of the most damaging of the Seven Forces of Negative," said Lon-Zara; "yet it is easily subdued. To master fear, learn to see beyond it. Recognize some GOOD to come out of an experience of trouble and the fear of it will go. You must understand that there is only ONE POWER in the universe and it is good. Its three aspects you have already learned (Life, Love and Light). Now you must learn that you have TWO CHOICES to make in regard to the One Power. (1) You may attempt to BLOCK its action through ignorance of its true nature, and (2) you may USE it to bring about an environment or situation to which you can react pleasantly, and positively.

"If you are unwise and choose the first mode of action, the inevitable result will be unpleasant reactions such as Dis-Ease, Insecurity, and so forth. The One Power is still working but is being hindered and obstructed from its normal channels. This is the simple cause of most of the troubles of mankind on Earth today. They are trying foolishly to CHANGE the natural action of this One Universal Power. However, the One Power cannot be changed for it comes from the Absolute. Man's, wrong use of it reacts adversely on himself.

"If you use wisdom and choose the second mode of action, you at once become a conscious cooperator in the GREAT PLAN, and then you will no longer suffer from the Forces of Negative for they will begin to vanish from your consciousness. Always remember that the One Power is always GOOD, even when it is being blocked by man so that it has to react negatively. For example, Sickness is good for you when you NEED it. It serves to help awaken you to Nature's laws of health. Wien you learn those laws and apply them, you get well. So you see the UNDESIRABLE NEGATIVE is good for you when you need it, but it still' better not to need it.

THE CENTRAL LIGHT OR DIAMOND STAR

"On Venus, all that your people of Earth consider negative, discordant and destructive has long ago vanished. Crime, Poverty, Wars, Disease, Old Age problems and numerous other unpleasant conditions do not exist on our planet. That is why we call it a "Positive World". Picture yourself living in a world that sees things AS THEY ARE instead of as they appear to be, and you will have some idea of the MAGIC LIFE that awaits you when you "graduate" to Venus. What is our secret? We have found the "DIAMOND STAR" within ourselves. Each of us-men, women and children-on Venus, has discovered that a CENTRAL LIGHT dwells at the center of our Being. This light is the Star of the True or Divine Will of the Universe. It is of the most intense brilliance,

THIS SIDE FOR STUDENT NOTES

like a great Diamond. Each Venusian is taught how to find the Diamond Star. Then he or she freely places his personal will in line with Its Guidance. To us, anything else would be unthinkable and most foolish. Thus we become active and conscious cooperators in the Universal Plan.

"Therefore, on Venus, you will find no negatives to retard your forward progress into the GREATER LIFE, LOVE and LIGHT that you have yearned and prayed for so long. As you have already guessed, the average Venusian builds his complete expression around the three primary principles, and he does this freely of his own choice. All actions spring from knowledge of these great universal principles. INTELLIGENCE is always placed before (given prime importance over) desire, so that desire becomes purpose, and each purpose is automatically in harmony with the Great Universal Will of the Creator of all. By putting Intelligence before power, the result is always constructive and beneficent. By putting power before Intelligence, the result is chaotic and destructive. Earthlings are only now learning this."

THE MAGIC OF POSITIVIZED INTELLIGENCE

"Is it really possible for humanity, even advanced beings such as your people of Venus, to so eliminate human errors that all their efforts are positive, constructive and in harmony with God's Will?" I inquired.

"Millions of years ago," Lon-Zara began, "before the long and benevolent reign of Sanat Kumara and his Lords, our world was quite similar to your planet Earth. It was both Negative and Positive in its activity and expression. Our people had not yet learned the secret of HOW TO LIVE from a "Divine Center" within themselves. We did not realize consciously that a Positive world demands the development of Positive Intelligence, What is "Positive intelligence"? It is simply the use of your reasoning faculties to guide and direct the two universal forces of LIPE and LOVE constructively, so that the result will benefit humanity rather than bring injury, suffering and death to it.

"On your planet Earth, Divine Love is not recognized, and fear rules mankind. Why? Because in place of recognizing LOVE as one of the primary universal principles and becoming channels for its healing, harmonizing and sustaining power, the majority of Earthlings have substituted the LAW OF FORCE. Each man and woman seeks his or her own happiness, and forgets the existence of others. This is contrary to the COSMIC PLAN, for we know that each human being is like unto an individual

THIS SIDE FOR STUDENT NOTES

brain cell of the SUPREME BEING, and by means of an inconceivable number of human beings on planets throughout the COSMOS (in our Galaxy alone, the Milky Way, an estimated 20 million planets are inhabited)   the ONE UNIVERSAL MIND IS manifesting Itself.

"Under the spiritual guidance of Sanat Kumara, the first Lord Thinker of Venus, our people at last saw the wisdom of living in tune with the Universal Plan, which required man to THINK and GUIDE the forces of LIFE and LOVE which already existed and were eternal in nature. What was the need of taking things by force from others? All we needed to do was PICTURE IN OUR MINDS the good things of life, and BELIEVE in the law of LOVE. To us, this meant harmonious, constructive and CREATIVE ACTIVITY. An abundance of good things was thus easily produced, and wisely distributed by an economic system that requires no money, no trading, no exchanging of anything – It is neither Communism nor Socialism – but a far superior system to anything the Earth has ever known. Not even your best utopian dreams had our plan.

"What was the use of hurting, deceiving, killing our fellow human beings, or taking the lives of animals for food? We saw that ALL of these life forms are part of ONE GREAT LIFE, in essence our own life. Why should we hurt and kill ourselves? We learned that LOVE never takes things apart; it only adds to them and holds them together in line with the COSMIC PLAN."

"Then," I said, "your great secret is to live, create and build in conformity with the principles of Universal Will?"

"Yes...that is it. Venusians know that any other path is but an illusion—Let me describe our Cities to you. They are designed simply and in harmony with the structural principles of physical atoms. An atom has only ONE central nucleus from which the greatest positive LIGHT radiates out to the several electrons revolving about it. Venusian supreme government is based on this pattern. We have but one mighty Executive Center for the whole planet. At this Center, which is composed of three great circular, dome-shaped buildings made of a special crystalloid material, the Lord Thinkers dwell. They are masters of VITICAL FORCE and are motivated solely by Love and Light. Their Intelligence, Executive Ability, and Soul Quality are the highest of all the beings on our planet.

"Extending outwards from this Central nucleus, like spokes radiating out from the hub of a wheel, are eight magnificent highways leading to eight great cities. Each of

THIS SIDE FOR STUDENT NOTES

these Cities has four highways of its own, leading to four other cities, and each of the four cities has two highways leading to two cities. This pattern is continued around the planet."

"How interesting," I said. "Would you tell me something of the physical features of your planet and something of the customs of your people? I have supposed that your planet resembles the Earth in many ways."

"It does," said Lon-Zara, "with the exception that Venus is far more highly electrified than the Earth, and contains a greater relative proportion of radio-active matter within its nucleus or core. This causes our planet to emit a halo of radiant matter from its north and south poles. There is, however, nothing fiery about this self-emitted planetary light. It is a phosphorescent glow similar to the Aurora Borealis and Australis (Northern and Southern Lights) produced on your own planet Earth. The radiance is not hot, but cool. If you were in a spaceship at a height of 2,000 miles above Venus you would see this tremendous halo of brilliant light. It rests like a shimmering, rainbow-colored blanket over our peaceful world. At a distance of about 300 miles above the surface of Venus, this blanket of light merges into darkness. Yet beneath that light you could see the whole sphere of Venus illuminated not only by its own halo of self-emitted radiance, but also by the daylight produced by solar energy. The coloring of the cloud masses is breathtaking in effect. Gorgeous hues of iridescent colors and tints give the land areas below a spectacular beauty, far transcending that of Earth.

WHY VENUS NEEDS NO MOONLIGHT

"By day, this halo of self-emitted radiance about Venus becomes invisible, by reason of the overpowering brightness of the light produced in its atmosphere by electric energy from the Sun. But by night it becomes visible as Aurora, and provides a continuous light equal to that of the full moon on Earth. It is for this reason Venus has no moon, and needs none, for at night its light is supplied by its own self-luminosity."

"Does the luminous halo around Venus obscure your view of the stars and other heavenly bodies, from the surface of the planet"? I inquired.

"Scarcely at all, not more than the light of the Earth's moon obscures the stars from the people on Earth. Now relax for a moment; hold the Telolith Stone to your forehead, and I will show you a view of our planet via MENTA-VISION."

THIS SIDE FOR STUDENT NOTES

I did so, and suddenly the full glorious scene burst upon my "mental screen". I could see the surface of Venus clearly as though I were above and looking down at it. I watched, spellbound by the beauty of the awesome sight. Great mountains, forests and valleys were revealed to my mind's eye. The coloring of everything was magnificent, with pastel pinks, greens, yellows, and blues predominating. Oceans, rivers, and lakes much like ours, but the coloring differed. Lush vegetation covered the great valleys. I saw that the homes and buildings were constructed differently than ours. Homes were mostly single-story dwellings located some distance from the cities. The design was not always the same, but circular dome-shaped homes seemed to predominate. These appeared to be made of some kind of translucent crystal or plastic substance. Each home occupied a large, individual area of land.

I noticed that many people built beautiful homes on the mountainsides, similar to our custom in the Hollywood Hills of California. A great network of highways was observed, with numerous vehicles moving at tremendous speed over them. Most impressive to me were the spacecraft that dotted the skies above the planet. Some were cigar-shaped, some spherical like a miniature planetoid, some bell-shaped, and some in the simple shape of discs. In size, some of the wondrous vehicles exceeded 1000 feet in diameter. This, then, was my visual impression of Venus. In comparison to the Earth, Venus has more land area; while the Venusian oceans, though deeper, cover a somewhat smaller proportion of the surface.

The scene was thrilling beyond words, but lasted only a few moments and then faded out. Lon-Zara spoke.

"Creative activity is the keynote of our planet. There is no reason for our people to be idle, bored, or discontented; for each individual knows that he or she is an Integral part of a great and noble CAUSE. The system, like man himself, is in a process of ever-becoming more and more perfect. However, the basic structure of our system is built upon universal principles In the same way that an atom is built. It is for this reason that CIRCLES predominate in all of our buildings, cities and in our spacecraft. Venusians as a race of people are highly industrious, but in an artistic and deeply creative way. Our system develops more real INITIATIVE in the people, stimulates them to serve and uplift one another by giving them an INCENTIVE far more powerful than money. I shall explain here briefly that this incentive is a quicker promotion to the Kingdom of the Sun, for those who serve most abundantly. This is a more glorious reward than any money.

THIS SIDE FOR STUDENT NOTES

"Each man, woman and child of Venus realizes great benefits through service rendered in relation to others...but you must understand that this service is not in any way compulsory but voluntary. And it is mostly mind and soul activity. Free Energy-derived from Solar Light Energy-provides our entire planet with power that has no limit and costs nothing except the VITIC effort required to channel and direct it.

"The land vehicles you saw on the highways of Venus are powered by magnetic light engines. They are absolutely silent and carry a force-field of energy which protects the passengers against accidents, even at tremendous speeds.

"There are no jails on Venus, since crime is inconceivable to sincere beings whose soul development matches their mental and physical development. The Lord Thinkers require what we call 'Trinity Ratings' of each citizen several times yearly. This shows the following data: (1) Intelligence or 'IQ', (2) Executive Ability, and (3) Soul Progress. Persons whose Soul Progress Rating falls below a certain level are given special assistance so that the Rating is increased.

"We have no hospitals on our planet, for each man and woman has his own 'Doctor within', and relies implicitly upon that healing force to keep the balance always in favor of health. Our very way of life builds positive health, for we live mostly outside in the sunshine and fresh air. And we eat foods that have been super-energized by the sun. Our food comes primarily from tree crops which provide us with a variety of sub-tropical fruits, nuts and, yes, beneficial teas. No animal foods are used except honey, for there are no cattle on our planet. Nor are there any carnivorous animals of any kind.

"Animals are not used for food or for service by Venusians. Our world has an abundance of seed-eating song birds with beautifully colored plumage. Also our planet has industrious, useful insects such as the bee and ant. (Author's Note: The bee and ant were brought to the Earth by Sanat Kumara, Lord Thinker of Venus, 18,000,000 years ago.)

"Although we have no hospitals, as such, on Venus, we do maintain special HEALING CENTERS wherein the individual is taught the power and application of LIFETRONIC HEALING, as well as the use of Color, Sound (Music and personal key vibration or ray) and Perfume. Lifetronic Healing pertains to a MENTAL method of healing one's own body or that of another, by means of 'Life-electrons' and Life-Vitrons which are universally present in all space. A veritable stream of these 'energy units' can be so directed mentally, that they will flow at once into the body or out of it

THIS SIDE FOR STUDENT NOTES

VENUSIAN HEALTH SCIENCE & VENUSIAN SECRET SCIENCE

at the command of the healer. Lifetronic Healing has superseded 'Materia Medica' and surgery on Venus; for by our mental direction of 'Life- trons' we are able to alleviate pain, restore physical and vital balance, and heal wounds instantly.

"Now, Michael X," said my Cosmic Teacher, "we shall discontinue our telepathic communication for tonight. Tomorrow evening I shall reveal much new information to you. It will relate specifically to the strange and powerful phenomena of SOUL POWERS now possessed by the highly developed Venusians. Ponder carefully the steps we have covered up to this point, for the next step will be truly understood only when you have mastered the teachings you have already received. I bid you good night, Beloved Friend."

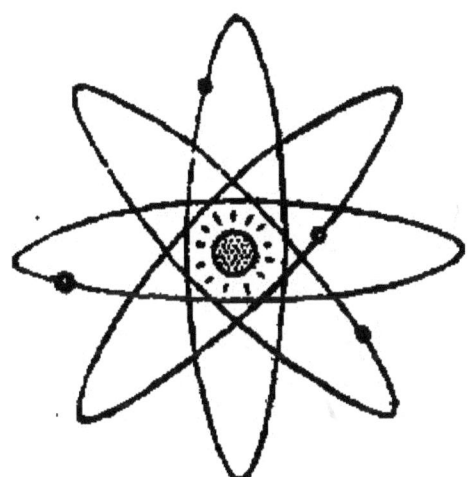

The Cities and Government on Venus are designed to conform to the laws and structure fond in the physical atom.

THIS SIDE FOR STUDENT NOTES

SPECIAL QUESTIONS

The theme of the Fifth Lesson suggests the following five important Questions:

1. What is the good result of being more orderly and harmonious in your personal life?

2. For vital New Age Health, should you include in your daily diet foods that have been pickled, roasted, toasted, boiled, frozen, dehydrated, pasteurized or fried? Give reason.

3. Is the One Power in the Universe ever "evil"?

4. What is the "Diamond Star" and where may it be found? Why does it resemble a Diamond?

5. What is the great secret of Venusian life?

THIS SIDE FOR STUDENT NOTES

VENUSIAN SECRET POWERS
Lesson 6

IN accordance with Lon-Zara's suggestion, I made a careful "review" during the next day, of all that I had been taught regarding the SECRET-SCIENCE thus far. To my astonishment and delight, I discovered that my ability to grasp and understand the important rudiments of the science had greatly increased. There was a directness arid simplicity to this new way of thinking, living and loving. I felt that I was soon to receive new and greater revelations from Lon-Zara that would open up to me startling and unrealized vistas of the powers dwelling within each true child of Nature.

That evening, contact by Telethot was again resumed with my teacher from Venus. Because I sensed that this new "lesson" would be on the vital subject of Venusian Soul Powers, and their practical methods of development, I had prepared a number of questions which I asked of Lon-Zara. The answers he gave to these questions proved to be not only quite astounding, but most interesting and enlightening as well. I have listed the Questions and Answers by number for your convenience in studying them.

MAGIC OF THE TWO PRIMAL ELEMENTS

Q. 1. "You have previously mentioned the two Primal Elements, Electricity and Viticity. Am I correct in believing that these two Primal Elements are the basis of all material and mental phenomena?

A, 1. "It is so, Beloved Friend. All things, both inanimate and animate – all matter, mind and soul – are made up of the two primal elements, Electricity and Viticity; and these in their ultimate nature are units of vibratory energy or if you prefer, vibration of the One GOD-SPIRIT."

Q. 2. "What is the source of these universal vibrations?"

THIS SIDE FOR STUDENT NOTES

A. 2. "The Great Central Sun at the vortex or hub of the Cosmic Universe, under the mental direction of the Supreme Being, revolves in space. In revolving, it produces electrons and vitrons which move outward from the center to fill all of space. Space is charged with these two Electric and Vitic units of vibratory energy, and since the Great Central Sun is constantly turning on its axis, more and more energy units are being produced. Hence the Cosmic Universe, though finite, is ever expanding."

Q. 3. "What is the characteristic quality of each of these two Primal Elements? Also, how may I understand the separate functions of Electricity and Viticity?

A. 3. "The two primal elements each have the quality of ENERGY. This is due to the fact that the units of Electricity and Viticity, namely the electrons and vitrons, are in a state of continual vibration. Now let us see what causes electrons and vitrons to vibrate. The electron (unit of Electricity) is always polarized into positive and negative forces called 'ions'. The unit of Viticity, the vitron, is polarized into positive and negative forces called 'vions'.

"The positive ion of Electricity is attractive in force, and the negative ion is repulsive in force. But the vions of Viticity show a REVERSE polarization. The positive vion being repulsive and the negative vion being attractive.

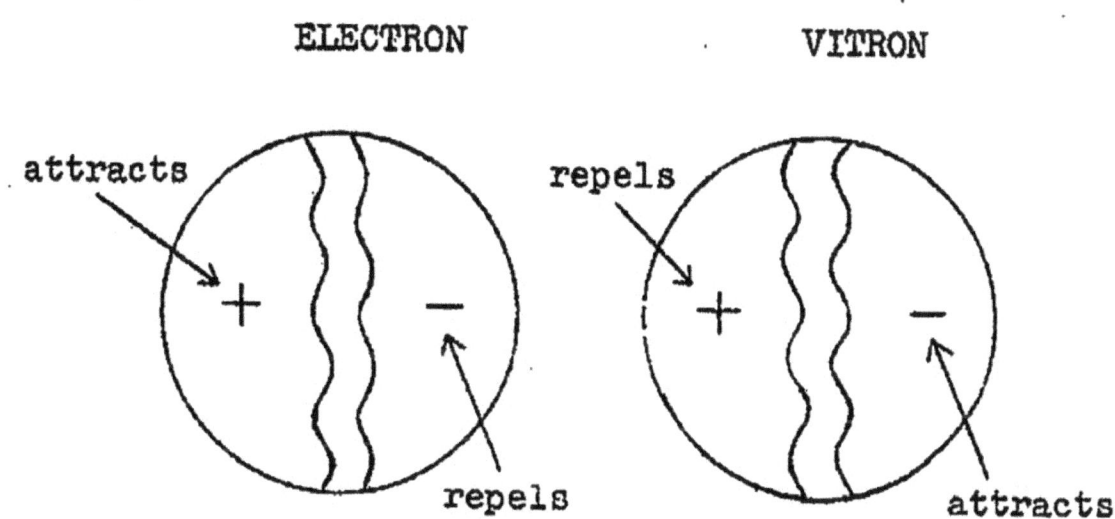

THIS SIDE FOR STUDENT NOTES

"The two opposing ions of Electricity in the electron are never entirely separable, and so are in constant agitation, waging as it were, a kind of warfare. This continual agitation of the opposing forces (attractive and repulsive) in each electron constitutes 'Electronic vibration'.

"It is important for you to know that the opposing vions in each unit or vitron of Viticity are likewise never entirely separable. Hence they also are incessantly exerting upon each other their opposing energy, thereby causing the phenomenon of VITIC FORCE, or 'vitronic vibration'.

"If an electron acquires a larger number of positive (attractive) ions, and has a smaller number of negative ions (repelling), then it is known as a Positive Electron. But if an electron accumulates more negative ions than it has of positive ions, then it becomes a Negative Electron.

"This applies also to the vitron. If a vitron has a greater quantity of positive vions in proportion to negative vions, then we call it a Positive Vitron. If it accumulates more negative vions than positive, we term it a Negative Vitron. In nature, that is, Universal Space, these two primal elements of Electricity and Viticity produce phenomenon which is either positive or negative in effect. Electricity for example, causes two different kinds of electrical phenomena according to whether the electrons are positive or negative. On Venus, Electricity is classified thusly:

THIS SIDE FOR STUDENT NOTES

PRIMAL ELEMENT
ELECTRICITY

(+) Positive Electrons	(−) Negative Electrons
Attractive Electronic Vibrations	Repulsive Electronic Vibrations
PERMANENT PHENOMENA	INTERMITTENT PHENOMENA
Magnetism	Light; including sunlight, starlight, planetary daylight and the Aurora Borealis
Gravitation & Weight	
Momentum	
Cohesion	Zodiacal Light and comets tails
Adhesion	
Chemical affinity	X-Rays
Volcanic action	Levitation; this has to do with the sustaining and retention of the heavenly bodies in their orbits, so they do not fall upon the Sun, or approach too near to other space-worlds.
Earthquakes & uplifts	
Ocean currents	
Atmospheric storms	
Weather conditions	
Movements of Suns, Stars, planets and other heavenly bodies in space	Cleansing of the atoms which constitute the human physical organism. Negative electrons can be directed by VITIC FORCE of the human mind, to repulse old, worn-out cells out of the body. This aids in healing.
Most physical and motor action	
Creation of all matter	
Expansion of the human body	

THIS SIDE FOR STUDENT NOTES

"You will at once note that the phenomena of Electricity whether positive or negative, are all PURELY PHYSICAL in character; whereas the phenomena of Viticity are always MENTAL, VITAL and SENSORY in their effects, VENUSIAN SECRET-SCIENCE classifies the phenomena of Viticity as follows:

```
                    PRIMAL ELEMENT
                       VITICITY
       (+)                |                    (-)
   Positive Vitrons       |              Negative Vitrons

      Attractive                             Repulsing
   Vitronic Vibrations                    Vitronic Vibrations
```

PERMANENT PHENOMENA	APPLIED PHENOMENA
All life in its higher or more highly animate state. This includes all of the numerous levels of life found in the vegetable, animal and human kingdoms.	The Conscious Mind
	Subliminal Mentality
	Thought & Thinking
	Feeling, Sensation
The human soul or Soul-Mind. Also termed Subconscious-mind or the Innate-mind in man.	Emotion, Hypnotism
	⎧ All Mental Action, including Telepathy, Prayer, Clairvoyance (Mental Television) Clairaudience or (Mental Hearing) Clairsensience or (Mental feeling as in Psychometry) Clairodorance or (Mental Smelling) Clairsavorance or (Mental Taste)
Subconscious Memory	
Subconscious Intellect	
	Lifetronic Healing
Creation of Life, its conception in an entity	Teleportation
	Materialization and dematerialization
*	⎩ Occult Levitation
*	
*	Death & Soul Transference; Reincarnation
*	
*	Mental direction of Physical Forces
*	

(SOUL-POWERS OF ADVANCED HUMANITY — bracketing the applied phenomena from "All Mental Action" through "Occult Levitation")

THIS SIDE FOR STUDENT NOTES

Q. 4. "Electricity then, is, broadly speaking, the substance of all matter?"

A. 4. "Yes, and the second primal element, Viticity, is the substance of all life, mind and soul."

Q. 5. "Do the two primal elements mingle with each other in Nature, or do they remain separated from each other?"

A. 5. "They always accompany each other and are always united and commingled in greater or less proportion. Just as the positive and negative ions in an electron are never entirely separable from each other, likewise the ELECTRON and the VITRON are never entirely separable. Together the tiny but powerful units of Electrical and Vitical energy-the electron and the vitron-perform their different functions throughout the Universe, and together they create and constitute all that is."

USE OF MIND WITHOUT THE LOVE— FORCES OF THE SOUL NEVER LEADS TO MASTERY

Q. 6. "What happens when Electricity preponderates over viticity in any form of matter or phenomenon?"

A. 6. "When the accumulation of electrons exceeds that of vitrons, the two primal elements manifest as 'Electro-vitrons'. Conversely, if the proportion of viticity is increased so that it preponderates over electrons, then the electro-vltrons are at once converted into 'vitro-electrons'. On Venus, we have discovered that the converting of electro-vitrons into vitro-electrons may be accomplished by MENTAL CONCENTRATION and the direction of elemental SOUL-FORCE; namely the Positive, Attracting VITRONS. Thought-force alone can move nothing. Soul-force must be utilized in all higher creative processes. When the mighty Avatar Jesus came to your Earth, he revealed this truth to you when he said, 'Which of you, by taking thought (alone) can add one cubit to his stature?' Herein we find the cause of most Earthmen's misfortunes. He imagines that thought-vltrons are more important to him than soul-vitrons. This is quite a serious mistake as he shall come to realize."

Q. 7. "Can you reveal to roe the essential differences between an Earthraan and a Venus man?"

A. 7. "The difference is primarily in the degree of SOUL POWER and WISDOM possessed by each being. The average Earthling does not live from his or her true Soul

THIS SIDE FOR STUDENT NOTES

Center. Instead, he worships the false gods of POWER, PASSION and PRIDE. You see, the qualities of Power, Passion and Pride have two aspects, one is destructive and the other constructive. Those Earthlings who worship MATERIAL POWER as exemplified by the atomic bomb, guided missiles, guns, etc., and who display a PASSION for remaining ignorant of the higher laws of the Universe, and who take great PRIDE in their ability to Injure or kill other living creatures, are using the destructive or negative aspects of the great trinity. This results in conditions which you would term HELL.

"If the human rulers of Earth, and the mass-minded, would reverse their attention from the negative to the positive aspect of Power, Passion and pride; by desiring the power of LIFE more abundant, and developing a worthy passion for LIGHT of Cosmic Wisdom, and taking a genuine pride in their ability to LOVE and sustain all of God's creatures, they would thereby manifest the New Age conditions of HEAVEN on Earth.

"Earthman is far overbalanced in his development of 'Material Power, Passion and Pride', and considerably under-developed in 'Soul-Power, Passion and Pride'. The first is the negative or destructive aspect, the second is the positive or constructive aspect. We may illustrate this by picturing a simple balancing scale, as follows:

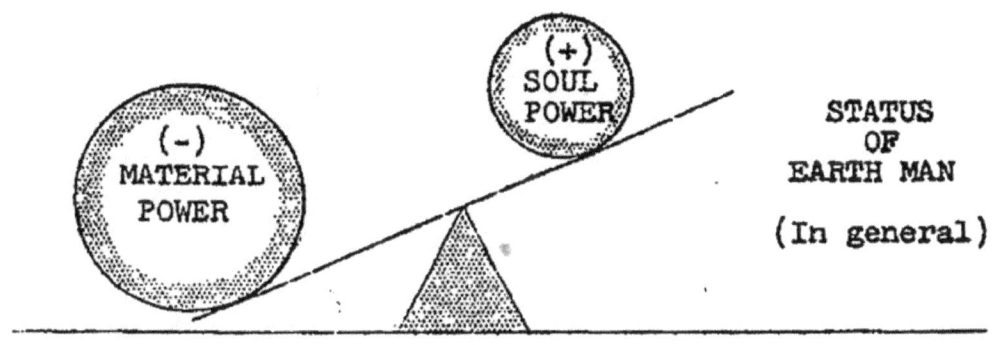

"Now let us illustrate the status of VENUS MAN:

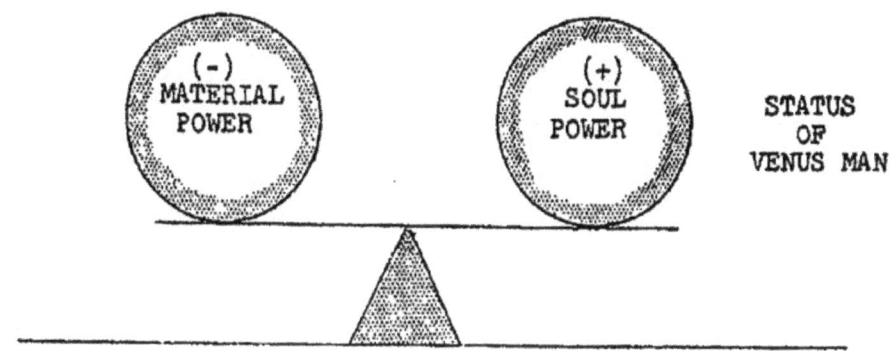

THIS SIDE FOR STUDENT NOTES

"Notice that VENUS MAN has greatly increased his SOUL POWER enabling him to wisely govern and BALANCE material Power.

"The spiritual aspects of LIFE, LOVE and LIGHT are well understood by Venus Man, and are expressed through the higher SOUL QUALITIES, or powers. Hence, Venus Man is able and ever willing to assist Earth Man in the unfolding of SOUL POWERS. For as you have seen, material power can only be balanced by the higher God-Sense (sense of GOOD). In this fact lies the special relationship that exists between Venus and Earth. We of Venus are one step beyond your evolutionary status, while the people of Mars are one step below your level. Mars cannot assist you in an upward direction, while Venus is able to."

Q. 8. "Will you describe briefly these higher powers?"

A. 8. "Yes; however, I wish to state first that every individual on Venus fully recognizes the divine origin of these SOUL POWERS, and is taught the proper use to be made of them. Also the manner In which to proceed for obtaining the required results so as to avoid all harm and obtain nothing but good.

"On Earth, the Conscious mind is deemed the 'normal' mind. But In truth, this phase of mind is extremely limited in its power to know and recall Information. Also, you will note (from diagram on Viticity) that the Conscious mind is obliged to draw upon the SOUL-MIND or Subconscious, for information contained In the Subconscious Memory and Intellect. The Soul-mind consists of Positive Vitrons which are attractive in nature, hence able to attract and tune-in upon negative vitrons anywhere in the universe. When Earth Man uses only his Conscious mind and ignores his Soul-mind, he is unable to accumulate sufficient vitic-force to demonstrate the higher powers of Soul. This blocks his Soul Progress.

"On the higher plane of intellect and mentality which prevails on Venus, the powers of the Soul-mind to reach out and acquire knowledge through the Central Senses are greatly enhanced. At the same time, however, the capability of the Conscious mind to assume and maintain the 'subjective state' (and thereby acquire and utilize the vast resources of knowledge possessed by the Soul-mind) is greatly increased. Thus on Venus the 'normal mind' more nearly approaches the SUBLIMINAL STATE OF MIND, or more simply, the subliminal mind.

"The secret science of Venus, in its ultimate sense, consists in the intelligent utilization of the Soul-mind by the Conscious mind. Startling SOUL POWERS as yet undreamed of on Earth, are manifested by Venusian men and women because all these higher

THIS SIDE FOR STUDENT NOTES

phenomena are a direct result of SUBLIMINAL MIND activity, and on Venus the Subliminal Mentality is well developed by all. In the Subliminal state, negative vitrons act upon the positive vitrons of the SOUL, which in turn react upon the electrons of matter. Thus we control matter.

"Now as to the actual powers, you are already acquainted somewhat with Telethot (Clairaudience), by which we are enabled to hear the sounds of things and voices of persons, not only far beyond the ordinary range of hearing, but from other planets millions of miles distant from our own. We also receive as by a voice speaking to us, answers to all sorts of questions.

"Menta-Vision (Clairvoyance) or the faculty of mental seeing, is very closely allied to Telethot; for these senses work in a similar manner. In Telethot, the Soul-mind reaches out by vitic induction, and brings back to the physical brain the vitical vibrations of the sounds and voices emanating from other persons with whom we are in mental attunement. In Menta-Vision, the Soul-mind ventures out (extends into space) by vitronic energy, until it comes Into vibratory attunement with similar vibrations of persons at any distant point in the Solar System. Then It brings back through reverse induction of the vitrons, a living PICTURE of absent persons, scenes or events that are transpiring at any location in the universe to which we direct our mind.

"We also make use of the faculty of Microscopic and of Telescopic sight. by which we are enabled to see the most minute and the most distant objects with the naked eye, as though we were looking at them with a microscope or telescope.

"Mind-Reading is one of the simplest mental phenomena, and is commonly practiced on Venus and on all the more advanced planets. All advanced Space-beings can read the thoughts of each other, thus making the mind an 'open book' to those who understand this process. Where the mind is an open book there can be no deception. Deception breeds fear. Venus has no fear because it has no deception and has developed such immense SOUL-FORCE that any outside evil can be NEUTRALIZED instantly by the Lords of Venus. Like all other mental phenomena, Mind-Reading is accomplished through the utilization of Viticity. It involves both telepathy and the reading of knowledge stored In the Subconscious of other persons (or a particular person). In this process, we project the vitronic vibrations of our own Soul-Mind into the Soul-mind of the subject, so that the vibrations of the two Soul-minds commingle with each other. We may then become conscious of and utilize the thoughts contained in the Soul-mind of another person.

THIS SIDE FOR STUDENT NOTES

"Our intellectual powers are vastly extended, by the manner in which we are educated on Venus. We learn all our lessons in the SUBLIMINAL STATE OF MIND, which does not weaken or in any way injure any sense, faculty or function of the oouter1 or physical being, but rather increases our powers and brings them to the highest degree of organic perfection.

"Students on Venus are able to record instantaneously, knowledge or data from any book by a process we call 'psychic-typing'. A mere glimpse, for a single second at any page in a book is sufficient for the students to retain in their memory the whole contents of it. By a slight extension of this faculty, the students obtain references from and even the perfect knowledge of, transcribed works which are known to exist in certain libraries at far distant places.

"The students are also able, by soul power, to identify themselves perfectly with everything belonging to the places spoken of in their study of Geography, Geology, etc., so that they feel as though they are on the actual spot mentioned. They appear to themselves to be, not where the lessons are conducted, but in the very places being studied; seeing, hearing and feeling all they are required or desire to see, hear or feel. This, as you will at once realize, makes the education of our young people of Venus the easiest of all things—real amusement and recreation—instead of being, as it Is now on planet Earth, a slow, tedious and fatiguing process.

"On Venus, for many ages, the principles of Levitation (overcoming of gravity) and Psychokinesis (moving of material objects by mind) have been commonly applied for such practical purposes as in the lifting of heavy and ponderous bodies; in excavating and removing soil and rock for structural building, in personal transportation of a limited nature where only the human body is used as the levitated conveyance; and in aerial navigation by means of small or large spacecraft."

THE MYSTERY OF HOW THE SPACESHIPS OPERATE

Q. 9. "Your Flying Saucers are not affected by the gravitational pull of planets, stars or suns?"

A. 9. "Each Space Disc creates its own artificial gravity by means of gyroscopic rotation and a force-field of Negative Electricity. Planetary gravity pull is thereby nullified. The source of ENERGY used to operate the disc comes from the SPACIAL ETHERS which as you now know, are composed of the primal elements: Electrons in combination

THIS SIDE FOR STUDENT NOTES

with Vitrons. By directing electrons from space to produce a force-field of electro-vitronic LIGHT, we generate para-magnetic (attractive) and diamagnetic (repulsive) forces which can and do impel the Disc at speeds approaching that of light itself. All that is necessary to move matter by thought force (vitic-energy) is to be able to accumulate a sufficient amount or 'potential' of that force. The great KEY to this problem lies in the use of special CRYSTALS that not only can accumulate vitrons, but focus and intensify their power as well. Spaceships are directed by VITICITY. Therefore the heart of every vehicle is its VITRONIC ACCUMULATOR. It is composed of a series of these CRYSTALS. They glow with a dynamic yellow luminescence when activated. What activates them? The vitrons which the Subliminal-mind of the Space-pilot directs into them from SPACE itself, using his own mind as the directive channel for the universal energy."

THE FREEDOM OF THE FREQUENCIES

Q. 10. "Is it true that Venusians are able to TELEPORT?" (dematerialize the material body and rematerialize it again at any other desired point in space .)

A. 10. "Yes, Teleportation is understood by the higher beings on Venus. It is, however, practiced only by our adepts who have attained to the higher frequency of the Fourth Density. At this level the Solar Body of the Adept has been completed but still not perfected. You will understand this more easily if I recall to your mind the various vibratory levels of frequencies of the human body. The grossest physical human body vibrates at the lower frequency of the Third Density. Such an Individual is very coarse, stupid and animalistic in his expression and appearance. As the vibrational frequency is increased or raised, the human body becomes more sensitive and its electronic matter becomes considerably finer. When the higher frequency level of the 3rd Density is reached by man, he is ready for life on Venus, where he begins on the Lower frequency of the Fourth Density of vibration.

"Venus Man then progresses upward from the lower frequency of the 4th Density to the higher frequency and then becomes a master of Teleportation. He or she is then ready for higher life on the next advanced planet, Mercury. The higher the vibratory frequency attained, the easier it is for a body to function in any particular Density. As you gradually progress up through densities 3, 4, 5, 6, you realize more and more freedom in your functional power. The final step is the 7th Density of vibration. This is

THIS SIDE FOR STUDENT NOTES

the high vibration of the Solar Body and must be achieved In order to take up your higher level of life upon the Sun."

After answering the above questions Lon-Zara terminated our mental communication for the evening. The subject of the next evening's lesson, he informed me, was to be "The Beings Beyond Venus". Who these Beings are, where they are located, and how they became the wonderful individuals that they are, would be made known to me. Moreover, humanity's true home—the SUPREME STAR—and some of its wonders, would be one of the important subjects of tomorrow's lesson. In a delightful state of joyous anticipation, I expressed grateful thanks to my Venusian teacher and retired for the night.

SPECIAL QUESTIONS

The theme of this Sixth Lesson suggests the following five Important Questions:

1. What is the name given to a unit of Electrical energy, and a unit of Vitical energy?

2. When Electricity consists of Positive Electrons it produces   phenomena.

3. When Electricity consists, of Negative Electrons it produces phenomena.

4. If Electricity is the "substance of all matter" what then is Viticity?

5. Material Power can only be balanced by   Power.

THIS SIDE FOR STUDENT NOTES

THE BEINGS BEYOND VENUS

Lesson 7

"**THE** Supreme Star" said Lon-Zara after telepathic contact had again been established on the following night, "is the home of the PERFECTED BEINGS of the Universe. Countless trillions of these Perfected Beings dwell on the Supreme Star at the very center or 'hub' of the galaxy. Tonight I shall tell you about those wondrous Beings, and how your own glorious destiny is to become a Perfected Being. First, however, I will reveal to you some vital information about the mighty Supreme Star, which is perhaps known to you as the Great Central Sun. What I am about to reveal is knowledge of great cosmic magnitude. Yet you will find it quite easy, to comprehend this teaching, for your mind and soul have been greatly expanded by the phases that have previously been given you.

"All the planets in our solar system revolve about a sun or 'fixed star', and all the stars revolve about the controlling Sun or 'Supreme Star' of the galaxy, in a tremendously vast field called the Galactic Plane. The Supreme Controlling Star is by far the largest and most highly electrified body of the galaxy. This is because it was the first, and hence is the oldest body of finite matter in the galaxy.

On Venus, we have computed the diameter of the Supreme Star to be about 120,000,000,000 miles, or about 165,000 times larger than our sun. In mass the central Controlling Star exceeds the combined mass of ALL the other heavenly bodies; just as the mass of our own sun exceeds the combined mass of all its planets.

OUR TRUE HOME AT THE HUB OF THE GALAXY

"The Supreme Star is by far the most perfectly adapted for the highest expression of human life of any bodies of the galaxy. It is so large as to seem almost a universe in

THIS SIDE FOR STUDENT NOTES

itself. It is the abode of 7th Density Beings-the highest grade of human development, both physical and mental, and is the plane of Omniscience, Omnipresence and Omnipotence. This means that the Beings on the Supreme Star have attained to a knowledge of all things, have annihilated space and time so they can travel anywhere in the universe instantly, and have the perfected understanding of all Cosmic forces and can direct by mental means all powerful energies in line with the One Universal Will of the Supreme Being."

"Do these Perfected Beings have physical forms like our own human bodies?" I asked.

"Indeed they do!" my Venusian Teacher replied, "They possess a glorified body which is constructed of Permanent Atoms from the Seventh Density. This is the substance of which the 'Solar Body' is built, and this body is not subject to death. It is immortal. In appearance, a Perfected Being is in the form of man, though taller and larger than Earthmen. Each Perfected Being is a distinct individual unlike all the other Beings, and is masterful beyond description. A powerful radiance of light surrounds the body of each of these royal and majestic Beings, and it is the combined intelligence of all the Perfected Beings which forms the Supreme Mentality at the center or hub of the galaxy.

"Each one of these Beings is a perfected expression or part of God, and exercises God-Powers by mentally controlling and acting as Guardian of great planets, stars and suns in the Universe. This great work is carried on under the mental direction and control of the first Perfected Being who is known as the Supreme Being. The Supreme Being is our Heavenly Father from whom all Human Life Waves originate. Since the point of origin for all humanity was the Supreme Star or Great Central Sun, we must each of us find our way back to that central point. We shall then be truly 'back home' with our true Father and all our glorious true friends, the Perfected Beings. Only then is man's pilgrimage ended.

"This goal," I said, "Is it to be accomplished by a gradual ascending of each human soul In an UPWARD progression via the SEVEN PLANETS and the SEVEN DENSITIES?"

"Yes, Beloved Earthling," replied Lon-Zara, "as human life advances from one planet to another, the Conscious mind comes more into vibratory rapport with the coordinate Soul-mind. The Soul-mind in turn, acquires more and more Intellect and power of understanding, until finally the Soul-mind becomes possessed of

THIS SIDE FOR STUDENT NOTES

Omniscience, Omnipresence, and Omnipotence. (Every Soul is seeking this Mastery.) When the Children of God shall have reached the 7th Density and become Perfected Beings of the Sun, their Conscious minds will then be capable of expressing their higher powers and of utilizing them wisely. Solar Citizens are then free to return to the Supreme Star if they so desire. This is the GREATEST REWARD bestowed upon a Soul: to travel HOME to the golden and magnificent Supreme Star, the greatest body in the galaxy!

OUR GALAXY IS A GIANT SPACE DISC

"This Galaxy, The Milky Way, in which our solar system is located, is shaped like a gigantic Space Disc. And, like a Space Disc, there needs to be a central intelligence within the Disc to operate and control it in space. This 'Controlling Center' is the Supreme Star, from which the Supreme Being applies the great mental force of Viticity to control all within this galaxy.

"Through the mental and soul-powers of the Supreme Being, the Supreme Star is caused to rotate upon its own axis, and through the mighty physical electro-dynamic effects of such rotation, all the other stars of the galaxy are propelled in their orbits around the Supreme Star. This causes them to rotate, in turn, upon their own axis, thereby extending the electro-vitic forces of the Supreme Sun throughout the Universe. Thus each sun helps the Supreme Sun distribute its light and energy throughout the galaxy.

"All is accomplished in perfect rhythm and with perfect precision under Supreme mental control of the Supreme Being and His assistants, the Perfected Ones, who direct the mighty motive and creative forces which are inherent as vibratory energy in the primal elements.

"By means of the Supreme Sun's electric and magnetic forces, applied through the process of its own revolutions upon its axis, each sun, planet and asteroid in the galaxy is rotated upon its axis, and moves with tremendous speed through the orbit in which the two opposing forces (attractive and repulsive electromagnetism) from the Supreme Sun maintain it. Each body in turn thereby becomes an 'electro' and 'vitro' magnet in the galaxy."

"Then these Perfected Beings," I said, serve the Great Plan by acting as Overseers or Guardians of the various planets?"

THIS SIDE FOR STUDENT NOTES

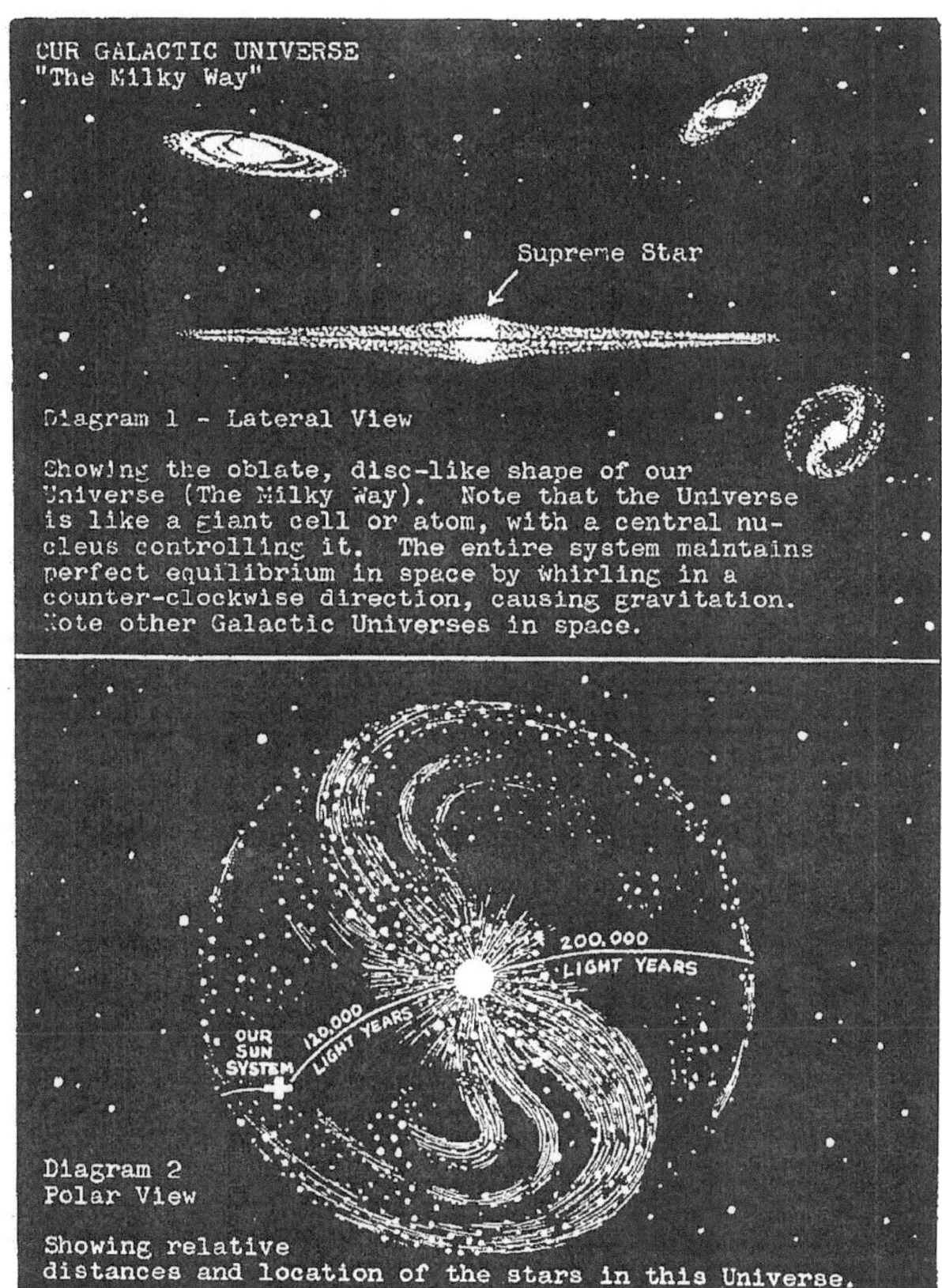

THIS SIDE FOR STUDENT NOTES

"They are greater than planetary Guardians," replied the Venusian teacher. "Planetary Guardians come from the suns of solar systems and from the next higher advanced planet in the system. For Instance, Venus is the home of the Lord Thinkers who act as Guardians of the Earth. It is for this reason that great Conferences are held on Venus periodically. Many higher beings attend these Cosmic Conferences; beings that live on our sun often appear. These are the principal planetary overseers. Perfected Beings who dwell on the Supreme Sun are Guardians of the Galaxy as a whole, and when they have served in that higher executive capacity for a sufficient length of time they earn the most glorious privilege of creating, energizing and ruling a complete Universe of their own. As you realize, the galaxy in which we live is only one of many such galaxies in space. Each must have its own central government of Intelligent, Perfected Beings.

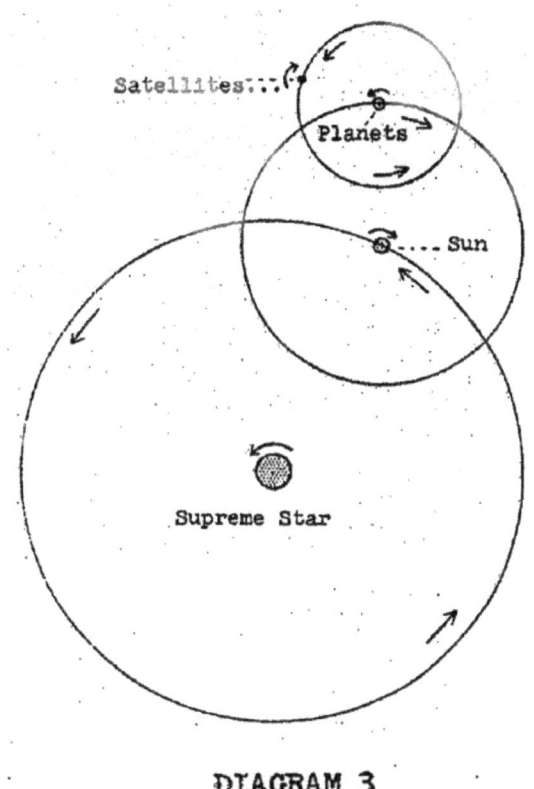

DIAGRAM 3

SYSTEM OF MOTION IN THE UNIVERSE

Showing the relative Axial and Orbital Motion of all the heavenly bodies of the Universe under the laws of Electrical Attraction and Repulsion.

THIS SIDE FOR STUDENT NOTES

"Are these Perfected Beings known as Masters?" I inquired of Lon-Zara.

"They are Masters of Matter and Life, but they are known as gods (spelled with small g) when they have attained to rulership of stars and sun systems and galaxies. What we think of as God (spelled with capital G) means the great assemblage of Perfected Beings in all the galaxies throughout the multiverse. This is the Supreme Intellect of the multiverse. Not one, nor two, nor three personalities, but a great multitude of Intellects who are ONE IN PURPOSE.

"This great assembly of GOD (Great Omnipotent Dynamo) is made up of all the perfected and matured human beings who have advanced from one planet to another through each succeeding grade of knowledge, and finally reached the Supreme Star, and in so doing have encompassed all knowledge and become Omniscient.

"This is our glorious destiny and reward. Every human being, as a 'child of God', after having lived a series of lives in human form upon ALL of the humanized planets in our solar system, and then upon the sun, will eventually become one, in knowledge with the Supreme Intellect. Each one of us will then participate, as one of the brain-cells of the Supreme Mind, in the further formation and direction of the multiverse.

"Upon reflection, it will be recognized that instead of detracting from the superlative character of God, this concept only serves to magnify the glory of the Divine Personality. For after all, the higher mind and soul of man is truly a 'living spark' of the Divine Spirit. And, in the light of this truth, all humanity becomes blended in unity. Would that they could all expand their conscious, understanding of the Great Plan.

"Now, Michael X, I bid you take these teachings and reveal them to your faithful friends, even as I have revealed them to you. Let each individual start at once, right where he or she now is, and bring LIFE, LOVE and LIGHT ever more abundantly into the daily life on Earth. Let LOVE be the guiding principle that opens all doors for you, heals all inharmonies, and lifts you into that higher consciousness where you become literally 'one of us'. Do not be dismayed by the vast extent of your Great Cosmic Journey. Take one step at a time; master that, and the next phase will unfold. Look UPWARDS always, never downwards. Continue to raise your personal vibrations to a higher frequency day by day by thinking of us and our Secret-Science. Apply our instructions to the best of your ability, and when the Great Day of Graduation arrives, we shall welcome you with all our love and Joy. On behalf of myself, Shelana, and the

THIS SIDE FOR STUDENT NOTES

Lords of Venus, farewell...unveil our science to Earth's humanity, now. When you have succeeded, we shall meet again."

With that, our contact by Telethot was broken and suddenly all seemed blank and empty before me. Deep within me, I knew that this feeling was only temporary. I would hear from Lon-Zara again. Until then, the glorious memories of my thrilling experiences...sighting the Space Disc, meeting both my Teacher and Shelana, seeing Venus by Menta-Vlsion, and so forth-would never be forgotten. Truly, there is no ceasing of wonders for New Age Individuals. What great adventures would shape themselves into .the coming months? Time and the Space-Beings held the precious secret. As you may well imagine, in spite of my fatigue, I did not go to sleep early this night. I walked up and down in my room, thinking over the events of each memorable contact. The mere thought of how greatly I had been privileged, moved me to the very depths of my soul. As I walked about the room I observed a Bible lying upon my desk. I did not remember placing it there. Obeying a strong impulse, I opened the Bible at random and my eye fell upon the second Chapter of Revelation to where it said: *"And he that overcometh, and keepeth my works unto the end, to him will I give POWER*...*And I will give him the MORNING STAR."*

THIS SIDE FOR STUDENT NOTES

SPECIAL QUESTIONS

The theme of the Seventh Lesson suggests the following five important Questions:

1. Of all the bodies in the Universe, which is best adapted for the highest egression of human life?

2. What kind of beings live upon the Supreme Star?

3. Who are the Guardians of this Earth?

4. What is the glorious destiny of every perfected and matured human being in our galaxy?

5. Who are the Guardians of this galaxy?

THIS SIDE FOR STUDENT NOTES

HERE ARE INSTRUCTIONS ON USING YOUR TELECRYSTAL WHICH CONTACTEE MICHAEL X REFERED TO IN HIS EARLY ENDEAVORS AS A "TELOLITH." INSTRUCTIONS FOR BOTH ARE IDENTICAL.

How Michael X Contacts The Space-Beings!

IN my search for a simple, practical and positive aid whereby I might contact flying saucer beings, as well as human intelligences living on other planets, I was led to the study and use of "Psychic Stones" or "Gems". By nature, my psychic or sixth sense is developed considerably beyond that of the average person (for which blessing X am most grateful), however, I have found that if one desires to reach mentally into outer space, and communicate with advanced beings by Telepathy, it is necessary to make use of every aid that will stimulate and increase one's telepathic power.

More contacts with Spacemen are being reported here in California than any other state in America, and in my opinion, this is due to the fact that a psychic stone, known as a TELOLITH, is being utilized by more and more persons here as an aid to ESP (Extra-Sensory perception) development. If you have never used a TELOLITH psychic stone, it is important to know something about the stone itself, what it looks like, where it may be obtained, end most important, HOW to use it for best results. I shall briefly describe the stone for you, and then give you the secret instructions for its use in Telepathic contacts. Bear in mind as you read that I attribute my personal success in "O.S.C." (Outer Space Communication) to my diligent and faithful use of a TELOLITH psychic gem. Of course, there are other Important secrets to observe if you are sincerely desirous of mentally contacting a Space-Being. These secrets will also be made known to you in this report, which, to my knowledge, is the first time this information has been made available to sincere seekers. May it open NEW DOORS of truth to you.

THIS SIDE FOR STUDENT NOTES

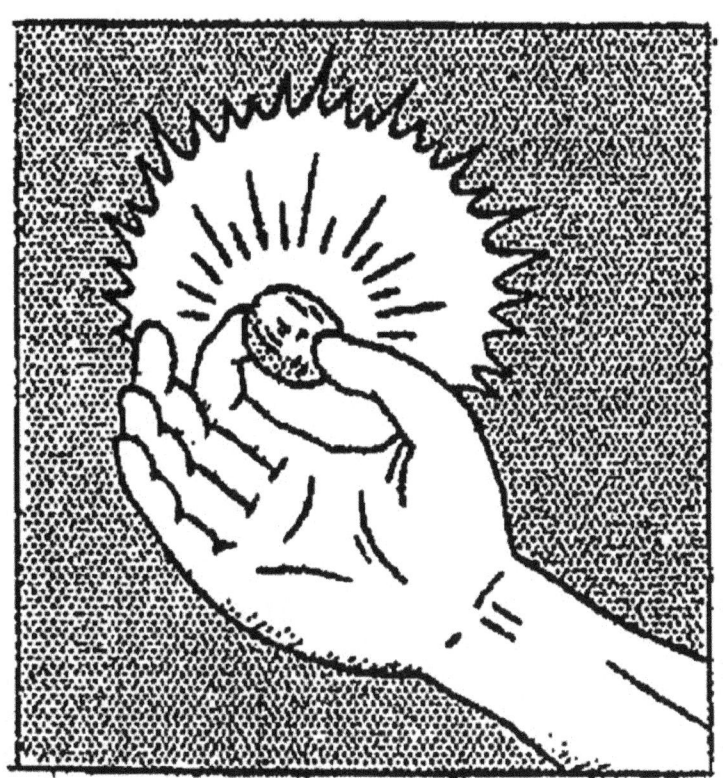

The TELOLITH is a rare boron crystal small enough to hold in your hand or carry in your pocket. It is translucent in appearance, usually in an unpolished natural state and may be of different shades of color depending on its environment. It is unlike most other stones in the fact that it possesses an enormous aura, or field of electro-vitic radiation. This aura around the stone, though invisible to ordinary vision indicates that the stone contains unique VIBRATORY QUALITIES. These vibrations from the stone are of a very high frequency, and for this reason the TELOLITH acts to "step-up" the sensitivity of your physical body (particularly the Pineal and the Pituitary glands which are the "psychic organs" so that you become wore easily and quickly "attuned" to the thought vibrations constantly being sent to Earth by the Space-Beings.

Therefore a psychic stone will prove a positive aid in the reception of "O.S.C." messages, when properly used. But that is not all. It will also serve to focus and intensify your own telepathic powers, thus enabling you to transmit to and also to receive the thoughts of the Space-Beings.

It is a well known fact that if you wish to project an electrical current to any distant point in space, you must first "step-up" the current to a higher voltage before you release it, otherwise there is no power to effect transmission. That is why I use a TELOLITH gem. It assists me to build up and intensify my MENTAL FORCES so they become very strong and positive. Other psychic gems may work as well as the Telolith for this purpose and are worth testing. Edgar Cayce, the famous psychic reader, advised the use of a stone called Lapis Lingua or "Singing Stone". Whichever stone you may prefer, the same instructions for its use will apply.

THIS SIDE FOR STUDENT NOTES

Now for step-by-step instructions. They are not at all complicated, nor hard to follow, but each step is important.

1. CONSECRATION: Because the Telolith psychic stone has a positive-negative vibration, it is able to draw in as well as throw off subtle thought influences. It has passed through many hands before you obtained it, therefore you must first de-magnetize it, so as to banish all traces of the past vibratory influences which it contains. This is accomplished as follows:

Take the gem up in your hands so that the fingers and thumb of your left hand hold one end of the stone, while the fingers and thumb of your right hand hold the other end of the stone- Now hold the stone quietly and think strongly of your highest ideal of LIFE, LOVE and LIGHT, for five to ten minutes, This "demagnetizes" the Telolith of all low vibrations. After you have done this, set the stone down on a table and DO NOT TOUCH IT for ten full minutes. Above all, do not allow anyone else to handle the stone. At the end of 10 minutes, pick up the stone again, hold it as you did before in both hands, and breathe on it slowly. As you breathe, inject the full intensity of your mind and thought upon the stone, seeing in your "mind's eye" the words LIFE, LOVE, LIGHT as if they were being written, engraved or impressed on the Telolith stone. Do this for five full minutes. The Telolith is now charged with your own personal and highest vibrations- From now on allow no one but yourself to handle it, for strange magnetism will affect it negatively. Next comes the vital process of "Invocation".

2. INVOCATION: The Telolith is now ready for use in assisting you to raise and intensify your mental vibrations so that thought communication with the Space People will be possible. Invoking or calling the Beings is the next phase of this higher work. Invocation serves two purposes.

First it will attune you with the higher consciousness of the Space Beings. Secondly, it will help the world in general. I have learned that it is unwise to petition these higher beings for merely selfish or material reasons. Bequests should be only in regard to spiritual matters such as will advance the world spiritually. Also, an Invocation should never be made kneeling down, for the act of kneeling down lowers your whole vibratory consciousness, and may bring you into attunement with the lower worlds of beings. This is never desirable. The aerial spaces are thronged with countless intelligences, some good, pure, true, and celestial. Others are just the opposite. To reach the true and good ones-the high beings of Venus-your heart must correspond by Invoking only the good, true and beautiful for noble purposes.

THIS SIDE FOR STUDENT NOTES

Therefore it is best to stand upright, holding the Telolith in your right hand so it rests lightly in your open palm.

LOOK UP and address the Space-Being, or Beings; silently and mentally. Do not speak aloud, for the spoken word is too Earth-bound. Instead, let your thoughts be from without inwards, from the material to the spiritual. Think from within, upwards, and always silently. Remember, the Beings are master telepathists. And they are looking for the aid of sincere Earthlings. Here is the Invocation I use to contact my Space Master:

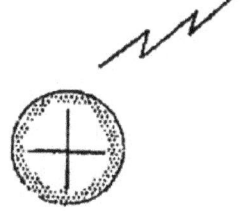

```
SPACE-BEING INVOCATION

"O Cosmic Teacher
of LIFE, LOVE and LIGHT
from the planet Venus
May the Spirit of Goodness
manifest on this Earth
as it does on Venus.
May the positive powers
of LIFE, LOVE and LIGHT
overcome all negation
and usher in the NEW
and GOLDEN AGE.

"Through the magic of Mind
reach out to me now
in THOUGHT communion,
that my soul may increase
in Cosmic Wisdom and Love
for the GOOD of all Life,
and the glory of the GREAT LIGHT!"
```

You are prepared mentally and spiritually for...

3. CONCENTRATION: Here is the method I personally use and which has proved most successful for me. When I desire to RECEIVE a message from outer-space, I hold the Telolith to ray forehead just above and between my physical eyes. This place is directly in front of the Pituitary gland, the psychic organ of telepathic reception. By exerting a moderate, firm pressure over this area, X find that the vibrations of the stone act to "step-up" the vibrations of the Pituitary gland, thus aiding my ability to CONCENTRATE mentally on outer-Space Communications.

THIS SIDE FOR STUDENT NOTES

When I wish to TRANSMIT or send a mental message to my Space Master, I raise the Telolith to the top or crown of my head, and hold it there while exerting moderately firm pressure. The spot is directly above the Pineal gland, which is the psychic organ of telepathic transmission. By applying gentle pressure to the Telolith at this spot just over the "third-eye", I find that the vibrations of the stone aid greatly in focusing and intensifying my thought-force so that I can transmit my own thoughts more positively and with a higher degree of success.

Another secret method I use, is something my own Teacher revealed to me and which is known only to advanced beings. It is called the "Awareness Slide". I have drawn three diagrams to illustrate this. The idea is to "slide" the focal point of your mental awareness (mind) between the Conscious and Subconscious areas of awareness, depending on whether you are sending or receiving a message.

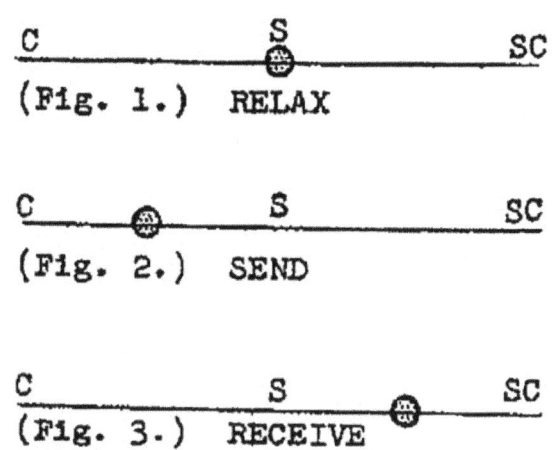

Fig. 1 shows a thread with a bead on it which can move in either direction from the center. "C" indicates the Conscious mind; "S" denotes the SUBLIMINAL MIND and "SC" refers to the Subconscious. Relaxation is needed first of all to enter the SUBLIMINAL STATE. Therefore I relax by holding a mental picture of the thread with the bead at the center of it, as in Fig. 1. Next, in order to SEND a message to my Space Master, I mentally move the bead toward "C" (Fig. 2) to allow my Conscious-mind to think of the thought I wish to project. As soon as I have formed the thought, I "slide" the bead back to the center promptly to point "S". From point "S" I mentally move the bead until it is between "S" and "SC" (Fig. 3).

Now I am ready to RECEIVE mental communications from my Space Master. This secret method of using the "Awareness Slide" together with the Telolith psychic gem should greatly assist you in your understanding of "O.S.C." and enable you, with devotion and practice, to succeed in your noble purpose.

Sincerely Yours,

Michael X

THIS SIDE FOR STUDENT NOTES

SUPPLEMENTARY INSTRUCTIONS

The Venusians embody love and wisdom. If you will seek to emulate those virtues and embody them in your soul and personality, you will find that after a while you will bring yourself into that state where you will naturally create an AFFINITY between yourself and your Venusian Teacher. Then, by your love, your intense devotion, you will in time draw him to you so that he will help you upward on THE PATH. But remember, Earthlings can never command the Venusians. Venusians are amazingly above Earthman, having more powers of every description. (See Lesson Six.) We, therefore, can never compel them through any kind of willful thinking or feeling.

By becoming more harmonious, loving and passive—and by consistent use of the Telolith or Lapis Lingua psychic stone—and having the proper attitude of devotion to the Wise Ones, it will be possible in time to draw them to you by magnetic soul attraction. Not to compel them in any way, but to win their appreciation sufficiently to accept you as a devotee of greater LIFE, LOVE and LIGHT; and in time they will appear to you. At first you will receive revelations and helpful messages from your Teacher during your nightly dreams. However, these dreams will not be like your ordinary dreams. They will be extraordinarily vivid and intense and impress you profoundly.

Whether or not you have as yet seen your Venusian Teacher, the fact remains that he does exist and is as real as you are. The Venusians (and the Mercurians) are actual living entities in masterful human form, and they have been helping Earthlings for countless centuries. Now let us sum up the elements that are most necessary to making a successful contact:

First: A firm faith in the existence of the Venusians.

Second: Intense devotion to their service.

Third: Positive love for them personally.

Fourth: A harmonious, natural and meatless diet.

Fifth: Great zeal in carrying out their instructions.

Sixth: Regular use of a Telolith or psychic stone.

Lastly: Infinite patience in personal soul development.

THIS SIDE FOR STUDENT NOTES

Contact will be made when your soul and its powers have reached the proper state of unfoldment. Do not seek to rush this, for it cannot be rushed. Be guided by these seven steps -banish all tendency to impatience-and like the rose, your soul shall unfold in great beauty. Be ready at all times to obey whatever prompting you receive from the Wise Ones; keep your faith firm, and by this attitude of communion and trust you may indeed be able to enter into communication with them in the wondrous and glorious NEW AGE of magnificent LIFE, LOVE AND LIGHT!

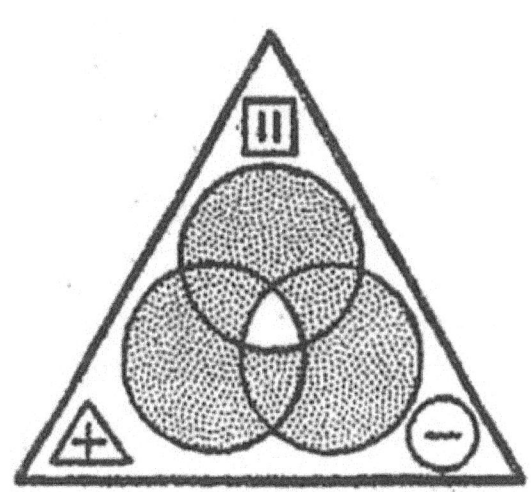

For our FREE catalog of books and other interesting items, send your name and mailing address to:

Global Communications
P.O. Box 753
New Brunswick, NJ 08903

Email: mrufo8@hotmail.com

www.conspiracyjournal.com

ALL TITLES AVAILABLE ON AMAZON.COM — PRINT AND KINDLE EDITIONS.

NORDIC LOOKING ALIENS GIVE HITLER PLANS FOR A TIME TRAVEL DEVICE!

THIS IS BY FAR THE MOST SHOCKING AND POTENTIALLY TROUBLING BOOK WE HAVE EVER PUBLISHED.
IT COULD VERY WELL CHANGE THE FUTURE— AND THE TRUTH IS—IT MIGHT HAVE ALREADY!

Here is disturbing evidence that Hitler had a top secret brigade of Nazi engineers working in deep underground laboratories – in conjunction with off world interstellar cosmonauts – to establish space flight and time travel, years before the start of America's rocketry program in which the U.S. sought the help of thousands of Nazi war criminals bought into this country under the auspicies of the tight lipped Project Paperclip. Information recently obtained by the authors indicates that the UFO that crashed outside Roswell might have been part of this Nazi space/time travel program cleverly covered up by our military in order to look like the arrival of an out of control interplanetary vehicle. The top brass was ultimately looking to cover their tracks which showed that they were inappropriately working in tandem with war criminals, whom they had excused of all evil misdeeds, eventually giving them citizenship. This "wonder weapon" and time travel device was named Die Glocke or "The Bell," and it is probably being seen and flown to this day; some even manned by Aryan- looking occupants (possibly Ets).

Devices like "The Bell" may have been used to bend both space and time and give the Nazis the unthinkable power to explore the past freely and even to CONTROL THE FUTURE. Are we plummeting headlong toward a world under fascist domination – a nightmare in which sadistic, jackbooted thugs are waiting for us to "catch up" in time with our own predestined subjugation to open worldwide rule by the Nazis, possibly hiding out on the surface of the moon or at "secret cities" at the Poles? Do they lie in wait for us as the clock on our freedom runs down?

The shocking facts can be read in **NAZI UFO TIME TRAVELERS** / Just **$20 + $5 S/H**

WANT TO READ MORE?

☐ **THE OMEGA FILES: SECRET NAZI UFO BASES REVEALED!**

Did Hitler's henchmen escape from Germany and set up secret bases at the South Pole and deep in the Amazon? Are they operating from these top secret quarters to establish a Fourth Reich and take over the world? – **$21.95**

☐ **UFOS NAZI SECRET WEAPONS**

Banned in 22 countries the author was imprisoned for over 20 years because he spoke out on this controversial topic. Did the SS have its own arsenal of super secret weapons which they planned to unleash? Here are pages of drawings showing these devices along with German plans of operation. – **$24.00**

☐ **THE SECRET SPACE PROGRAM**

Do we already have bases on the Moon? Who is responsible? Tesla? Nazis? Secret Societies? NWO? Something pretty damn strange is happening under our very eyes! – **$24.00**

FREE AUDIO CD OF THE MYSTERIOUS INTELLIGENCE OPERATIVE COMMANDER X TALKING ON THE NAZI UFO SPACE PROGRAM WHEN ORDERING TWO OR MORE TITLES FROM THIS AD. Special – All 4 books this advt **$79.95 + $8 S/H**

TIMOTHY G BECKLEY, BOX 753, NEW BRUNSWICK, NJ 08903

BERNIE SANDERS IS RIGHT ABOUT WALL STREET

FIND OUT WHY WHEN YOU READ WHAT SOME ARE CALLING THE MOST DANGEROUS BOOK IN AMERICA.
Breaks All The Rules! – Goes Against All The Systems!

In fact, the Vermont Senator has only grazed the tip of the iceberg when it comes to deceit and fraud in the banking and financial sectors. They are not just sucking your retirement fund dry. The truth is they are manipulating the politicians who take money from them and have secretly been financing our global conflicts since WORLD WAR ONE. They have become the richest individuals in the world off our blood, sweat and fears.

This hefty volume exposes a world of treachery, answering the questions: Who are the masterminds behind global domination? Who actually manages the flow of paper money and controls commerce and the banking system? Who really profits from war?

☐ **Order WALL STREET BANKSTERS – 334 pages. Large Format. $22.00 + $5 S/H**

AND IT DOESN'T STOP THERE!
☐ **FIGHTING THE FEDERAL RESERVE**

Here is the story of Congressman Louis T. McFadden the man who took on the Fed and was nearly assassinated when he boldly insisted that WW I, the Great Depression and World War II were events which were not desired by the American people, were not planned by the American people, and were not voluntarily entered into. But all of these events were instead the result of the planning of men who have no addresses, no fixed homes, and no substantial loyalties — save only to their own criminal interests.

Over 600 pages. $24.00 + $5 S/H

☐ **SPECIAL – BOTH BOOKS $34.00 + $6 S/H**
TIMOTHY G BECKLEY, BOX 753, NEW BRUNSWICK, NJ 08903

Radionics Boxes are custom made and may vary slightly from illustration.

FIRST TIME AVAILABLE CUSTOM MADE— AUTHENTIC MIND MACHINE THE RADIONICS BOX

Many have asked for this controversial box which it is said can be used multiple times to help manifest your desires in an almost "magical" way. However, the Radionics Box is based upon a strong foundation, whether you want to dramatically improve your finances, health, or relationships.

By setting your goal, and tuning your mind-body-environment relationship with the 9-knobs, stunning things can manifest. *VIRTUALLY WHATEVER YOU CHOOSE.* Thus, it must be used wisely. Some call this advanced "magic" or "techno-shamanism."

☐ *ONLY $250.00 FOR YOUR PERSONAL RADIONICS MACHINE AND WORKBOOK*

If you wish, our technician will customize the box for you! Along with your order, send us details of your innermost desire. This will ensure your box is designed properly for *you*. Our *MIND MACHINE* study guide will be included. Send payment of $250 to;

TIMOTHY G. BECKLEY BOX 753, NEW BRUNSWICK, NJ 08903

Note: Allow time for customizing. Since this is an experimental product, we **CANNOT** offer refunds or accept returns. PayPal and all other payment forms accepted.
Send email mrufo8@hotmail.com for PayPal requests.

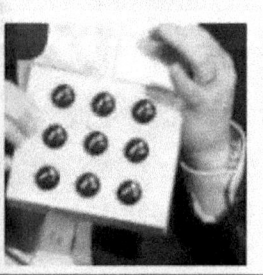

WE ACCEPT MONEY ORDERS · CHECKS · PAYPAL (mrufo8@hotmail.com) Credit Cards: 732-602-3407

REVEALED FOR THE FIRST TIME: THE TRUE IDENTITY OF THE MYSTERIOUS WHISTLE BLOWER KNOWN AS. . .

COMMANDER X

WILL THE REAL COMMANDER X PLEASE STAND UP!

NEW! – COMMANDER X FILES UPDATED

For more than a decade the mysterious Commander X has caused dissension among conspiracy theorists, Area 51 aficionados and UFO believers. Some accept his hair-raising accounts of working behind the scenes with the CIA, the NSA and other government and quasi-federal agencies at face value, while others scratch their heads in bewilderment and wonder if his first-hand chronicles cannot be linked to a disinformation program.

For the first time, here is the complete dossier on Commander X's many exploits both with various groups of highly aggressive ultra-terrestrials, as well as his battle with our own earthly authorities hell-bent on keeping these matters TOP SECRET! –

Included among the many shocking – and surprising – revelations in this book:

** The Alien Dinosaur Connection. – ** Who inhabits the Subterranean Regions of Earth? – ** Evidence suggests human victims were still alive, when their blood was drained and body parts removed in underground UFO bases. – ** The many special powers of ETs – including levitation, dematerialization, invisibility, mind control, advanced light beam technology. **A Nazi – Alien collaboration. How the Occult inner circle of the Third Reich contacted grey aliens before World War II using ritual magic. – ** Evidence Hitler shipped equipment and slave laborers to the Antarctic to construct a fleet of flying saucers. – ** Proof that the Nazis transferred into the midst of the American spy and space agencies.

AND MOST IMPORTANT OF ALL – ARE HUMAN CLONES GOING TO BE USED TO REPLACE ASSASSINATED POLITICIANS?

Only Commander X can dare answer these questions.

❏ Order THE COMMANDER X FILES - Large Format. 200+ Pages – $24.00.

❏ NEW! – AMERICA'S TOP SECRET TREATY WITH ALIEN LIFE FORMS – PLUS THE HIDDEN HISTORY OF OUR TIME!

Is The "Treaty" A "False Flag?" – Or Some CIA Sponsored "Smoke Screen?" They arrived without our knowledge or consent and told our military leaders they came in peace for the benefit of humankind, and would gladly start an exchange program with the people of the planet earth which could lead to a "Golden Age." We wholeheartedly believed them and agreed to the "Treaty" almost without any sort of protest. Then they began to abduct our women! Then they returned for our children! Soon after they began to rape the earth's resources! And it became apparent they ultimately wanted to control our minds and capture our souls for their selfish reasons, some too horrific to comprehend.

And because they are too embarrassed to admit they went along with this Treaty, the U.S. government and the military industrial complex refuse to let the public know what has been going on for nearly half a century, keeping a tight lid on this Treaty and its various "exchange programs." But now there might be a ray of hope thanks to the whistle blower known as Commander X. This is your opportunity to find out about the "Treaty," and protect yourself and your loved ones from a possible "enemy attack" that could come out of the sky, as predicted by Nostradamus, as detailed in the Book of Revelations.

Find Out The Truth For Yourself by ordering SECRET TREATY WITH ALIENS.

❏ Large Format – 186 Pages – $20.00.

❏ SPECIAL: BOTH NEW BOOKS BY COMMANDER X - $39.00 + $5 S/H

TIMOTHY G. BECKLEY, BOX 753, NEW BRUNSWICK, NJ 08903

MOST BOOKS ARE PRINTED IN LARGE EASY TO READ FORMAT, AND FULLY ILLUSTRATED

FASTER THAN THE SPEED OF LIGHT!

THE TOP SECRET SCIENCE OF TOMORROW IS HERE TODAY!

Time Travel
Teleportation
Dimension Jumping
Invisibility

THESE TITLES AVAILABLE BASED UPON CONFIDENTIAL INFORMATION DERIVED FROM KGB, CIA AND CHINESE WHISTLEBLOWERS

❑ NAZI TIME TRAVELERS

Whistle blower indicates UFO that crashed outside Roswell might have been part of a secret Nazi space/time travel program covered up by CIA to make it look like an out of control space ship crashed. The top brass were looking to cover their tracks in regard to allowing Nazi engineers and rocket scientists into the US illegally under Project Paperclip. Evidence Nazis had been in contact with Aryan space beings who assisted in developing an advanced "flying disc" technology on advice from members of a German secret society the Vril. —**$20.00**

❑ TIME TRAVEL FACT NOT FICTION

Einstein had part of the equation correct but did not consider what has become known as the "string theory" of physics which says that everything in the universe exists simultaneously. In this work by Commander X and Tim Swartz a variety of topics are discussed, including: Spontaneous Cases of Time Travel. — Mystery of Time Slips. — Doorways in Time. — People, Buildings and Towns From Beyond Time. — The Restaurant At The Edge Of Time. — Flight Into The Future. — Is Death A Jump in Time? — Are UFOs Time Machines? — Working Time Machines — Nikola Tesla's Time Travel Experiments —**$20.00**

❑ TELEPORTATION – HOW-TO GUIDE FROM STAR TREK TO TESLA

Commander X says it is possible to master the art of teleportation. The well-known phrase, "Beam me up, Scotty" now has a rational application, the term Teleportation actually having been coined by the world famous researcher of unexplained mysteries, Charles Fort. The author says he worked on a secret teleportation project inside Area 51 in which a "beam ship" did a bit of "dimension jumping" while he was at the controls. Book contains experiences you can participate in.—**$16.00**

  ❑ Add $13 for OFFICIAL U.S.MANUAL ON TELEPORTATION released by Air Force Research Laboratories.

❑ TRAVEL TO OTHER DIMENSIONS

Discover how to: ** Become One With The Light — ** Discover The Reality Of Other Dimensions and Planes — ** What You Will Find On The Seven Planes Of Existence — ** Traveling In And Out Of Your Body At Will — ** Entering The Region Of The Disembodied, And The Sacred Resting Place Of The Soul — ** Life And Work On The Astral. -** Find Out The Entities You Are Likely To Encounter. -** What It Is Like To Mingle With Disembodied Souls, and learn to contact the spiritual teachers.—**$18.00**

❑ LEVITATION AND INVISIBILITY

This book is NOT to be used for unlawful or immoral purposes! Can we learn to fly through the air with the greatest of ease? Is it possible to walk through walls or other solid objects? Now thanks to Tim R. Swartz and retired military intelligence operative Commander X, working in tandem with various sages, shamans and adapts, we are prepared to proclaim the secrets to fulfilling these mystical "dreams" are at hand. Contents Include: ++ The Quest For Instant Invisibility. ++ What Is In The Mysterious Mist? ++ The Realm of Invulnerability. ++ Prayers and Spells For Invisibility. ++ Spiritualists And Mystics Who Have Proven They Possess Incredible Talents.—**$21/95**

❑ SUPER SPECIAL
Everything listed on this page PLUS A FREE Audio CD just $89.00 + $8 S/H

TIMOTHY G BECKLEY, BOX 753 NEW BRUNSWICK, NJ. 08903

www.ingramcontent.com/pod-product-compliance
Lightning Source LLC
Chambersburg PA
CBHW062126160426
43191CB00013B/2204